PRAYERFULLY WAITING

A Catholic Grandmother's Prayer Journal

DONNA-MARIE COOPER O'BOYLE

PARACLETE PRESS

BREWSTER, MASSACHUSETTS

2021 First Printing

Prayerfully Waiting: A Catholic Grandmother's Prayer Journal

Copyright © 2021 by Donna-Marie Cooper O'Boyle

ISBN 978-1-64060-341-7

Library of Congress Cataloging-in-Publication Data
Names: O'Boyle, Donna-Marie Cooper, author.
Title: Prayerfully waiting : a Catholic grandmother's prayer journal /
  Donna-Marie Cooper O'Boyle.
Description: Brewster, Massachusetts : Paraclete Press, 2021. | Summary:
  "Grandmother's prayer journal is a prayer guide for a grandchild's first
  nine months of life and birth"-- Provided by publisher.
Identifiers: LCCN 2020017676 (print) | LCCN 2020017677 (ebook) | ISBN
  9781640603417 (trade paperback) | ISBN 9781640603424 (mobi) | ISBN
  9781640603431 (epub) | ISBN 9781640603448 (pdf)
Subjects: LCSH: Grandmothers--Prayers and devotions. | Catholic
  women--Prayers and devotions. | Fetus--Prayers and devotions. |
  Pregnancy--Religious aspects--Christianity. | Spiritual
  journals--Authorship.
Classification: LCC BX2353 .O266 2020 (print) | LCC BX2353 (ebook) | DDC
  242/.6431--dc23
LC record available at https://lccn.loc.gov/2020017676
LC ebook record available at https://lccn.loc.gov/2020017677

10 9 8 7 6 5 4 3 2 1

Published by Paraclete Press
Brewster, Massachusetts
www.paracletepress.com

Printed in the United States of America

GRANDMOTHER'S NAME:

DATE YOU FOUND OUT ABOUT YOUR UNBORN GRANDCHILD:

HOW YOU FOUND OUT:

APPROXIMATE DUE DATE:

HOPES FOR YOUR GRANDCHILD:

YOUR FIRST PRAYER FOR YOUR UNBORN GRANDCHILD:

Contents

Preface

God made sure that his Son, Jesus, had a grandmother. She was St. Anne. God also gave to children the gift of grandparents—whether or not they have gone to their eternal reward before the grandchildren came into being. Grandparents' faithful lives and memories can certainly have a considerable effect on future generations. Recently, on the feast of St. Anne and St. Joachim, Pope Francis tweeted, "Grandparents are a treasure in the family. Please, take care of them and let them talk to your children!"

Through God's grace, and a grandmother's prayerful example and involvement, that grandmother has the tremendous capability to powerfully nurture and shape her grandchild's conscience. I can attest to that fact as I am sure countless others can, as well. My grandmother, the only grandparent I knew (because the others had passed away before I was born), was a beautiful example of a Christian life well lived. She was a simple Polish prayerful grandmother.

As a small child, I often gazed at the sacred images decorating the walls of her humble home. Many a time I kept an eye on the beads of her worn rosary moving slowly through her aged fingers, and I observed her lively faith through interactions and conversations. I always felt a certain comfort and holy security in my grandmother's presence. Her smile and laugh would illuminate a room. The light in her soft eyes radiated God's love. Perhaps without knowing it, she etched a precious model of living faith upon my heart. Observing her steadfast faith, lived out within her large Catholic family, positively drew me closer to God. My grandmother's and my mother's holy yet simple examples certainly urged me to carry the faith into my own domestic church later on.

I don't think we will have any arguing here about a grandparent's ability to positively influence their grandchildren. Yet, we should know that grandparents also have that amazing ability, by God's grace, to be a prayerful instrument even before the grandchildren are born! I believe that we need to truly recognize the great gift and role we have in praying for grandchildren in utero.

As a grandmother-to-be, you are undoubtably thrilled over the blessing of your upcoming role. It may seem a bit daunting to become a grandparent, or maybe you are a veteran. Even if this is not your first time around, your unborn grandchild is certainly one of a kind. He or she is a beautiful, unique, and unrepeatable human being—what an incredible blessing!

Without a doubt, you are naturally interested in your grandchild's well-being and can be involved in his or her life even now. This grandmother's prayer journal offers a delightful and unparalleled opportunity for you to not merely sit back and wait for the wondrous arrival, but instead, to use this time wisely by *prayerfully waiting* for your grandchild throughout what can be a meaningful and powerful nine-month novena of prayer. A grandmother's prayers are of significant importance through every age and stage of a grandchild's development—they are amazing and lovely blessings that can help shape their future lives!

Prayerfully Waiting will take you month-by-month while you learn, discover, and note the development of your precious "grand-blessing." You'll be inspired with holy insights too. Spaces are provided for you to personalize this special unborn baby book, as well as lovingly to record your thoughts and prayers as you pray for your grandchild's first nine months of life.

From beginning to end, you'll be partnering with St. Anne, the grandmother of Jesus, to swaddle your unborn grandchild with prayer. You'll journey with Mother Mary, and all the saints, to prayerfully prepare for the little one's birth.

As I write these words on this holy day, I can't help but think of a young Jewish teenager, Mary of Nazareth, who immediately put her own needs aside and "went in haste" to the hill country to assist her older cousin Elizabeth, who was also carrying an unborn baby. That selfless love, that tender heart for loving service, can stir our own hearts to strive to emulate the Blessed Virgin's virtues as we ask our dear Lord Jesus to reside in our hearts while we reach out in love to help others.

May this book nourish your heart and soul! Enjoy every minute in *prayerfully waiting* for your grandchild!

DONNA-MARIE COOPER O'BOYLE
The Visitation of the Blessed Virgin Mary

How to Use This Book

ove page-by-page throughout your unborn grandchild's first nine months of life. Each of the nine chapters will speak about that particular month of the pregnancy. Read each chapter all the way through and feel free to go back to it often throughout the month for reminders, prayers, and continued inspiration. The "Holy Insights" section will offer spiritual food for thoughts to ponder. The "Praying with the Saints" section will provide additional inspirational teaching.

You can pray the special novena prayer each day of your grandchild's life in the womb as you swaddle him or her in your thoughts and prayers. You will choose when you'd like to record your reflection and your prayers on the pages of this book.

Enjoy the journey. It was planned by God for all Eternity.

Praying with Gratitude

"Before I formed you in the womb I knew you,
and before you were born I consecrated you."
—JEREMIAH 1:5

ithout doubt, God knew your grandchild before he or she was even a hopeful twinkle in their parent's eyes. Add to that, God has specific plans for your precious grandchild. He or she is extremely blessed to have your prayers right now while in the mother's womb.

No doubt, you are excited and grateful to be a grandmother (whether or not this is your first time). Yours is truly a sublime role and vocation. Your loving prayers, your holy example, as well as your involvement in your grandchild's life will certainly be a positive and wholesome influence.

Throughout this first month in the womb, strive to pray many prayers of gratitude for your unborn grandchild. And let's take a look at your grandbaby's progress thus far.

Discovering my Grandbaby's Developments

By the end of the first month of development, your grandbaby will be a quarter-inch long. Your grandbaby's heart, digestive system, backbone, and spinal cord have already begun to form. His or her placenta will begin to develop. Your unborn grandchild is now 10,000 times larger than he or she was at conception. Amazing!

In the coming weeks, your grandbaby will develop quickly. Over the next few weeks, the nervous system and organs will begin to develop. His or her heart will begin to beat at the end of this month!

My Hope and Prayer for My Grandchild
THIS MONTH

In my own words

_____

_____

_____

_____

_____

_____

_____

_____

_____

_____

_____

_____

_____

_____

Holy Insights: A Bright Beacon of Light

The Catholic Catechism teaches much about the Christian family and instructs that the virtues of faith, hope, and charity should thrive throughout the home. It says, "'The Christian family constitutes a specific revelation and realization of ecclesial communion, and for this reason it can and should be called a *domestic church.*' It is a community of faith, hope, and charity; it assumes singular importance in the Church, as is evident in the New Testament" (CCC #2204). Christian families are very important to society. They can be bright beacons of hope in a darkened world. The Catechism states:

> "The family is the *original cell of social life.* It is the natural society in which husband and wife are called to give themselves in love and in the gift of life. Authority, stability, and a life of relationships within the family constitute the foundations for freedom, security, and fraternity within society. The family is the community in which, from childhood, one can learn moral values, begin to honor God, and make good use of freedom. Family life is an initiation into life in society." (CCC #2207)

It's fascinating to consider that God has his mighty hand involved in choosing our family members. It's not just a random thing. Each of us, with varying personalities, strengths, and weaknesses, are together for a reason. A lot happens within the walls of our domestic churches. That's where families work out their salvation through the nitty-gritty details of ordinary daily life. Certainly, your family will not always resemble a page from the *Catechism* or *Butler's Lives of the Saints.* Probably, at times, far from it! We make mistakes, we lose our patience, we can even fail miserably. That's where the Sacrament of Reconciliation comes in, again and again. That's also where forgiveness and tenderness come in—over and over. We are all works in progress. However, we need to not only try our best to work out our salvation, but we need to strive for sanctity too. Yes, it's true. Even you! Even me!

Dear St. Teresa of Calcutta, whom I was blessed to know personally, would often state that holiness is not a luxury of a few, but a simple duty for us all. Let's be sure that our children and grandchildren learn about their faith and how to honor God from a young age. We need to strive to be exemplary models for them. Let them observe a vibrant faith shining from your eyes, being voiced from your heart, and lived lovingly through your actions. Begin now to be that vibrant example by praying for your unborn grandchild. Offer to God your heartfelt prayers.

Swaddling with Saint Anne

St. Anne is the mother of the Blessed Virgin Mary and the grandmother of Jesus. Anne was married to St. Joachim. She is often invoked for her intercession during pregnancies. The Catholic Church teaches that Anne was advanced in years and had earnestly prayed that God would grant that she could conceive and give birth to a child. One time as she prayed near her home in Galilee, an angel came to greet her. He said, "Anne, the Lord hath heard thy prayer and thou shalt conceive and bring forth, and thy seed shall be spoken of in all the world."[1]

Anne answered the angel with a heartfelt promise, "As the Lord my God liveth, if I beget either male or female, I will bring it as a gift to the Lord my God; and it shall minister to Him in holy things all the days of its life." Thus, Anne became the mother of the Blessed Virgin Mary. She is the patroness of housewives, women in labor, and surely every one of us who desires holiness in our children and grandchildren.

Each month you can invoke St. Anne to help your unborn grandbaby by praying the prayer below.

Swaddling with Saint Anne Prayer

Dear St. Anne, mother of the Mother of Jesus, I pray that I may unite my heartfelt prayer to yours and that you will present it before the throne of God. For so long you and Joachim prayed for a child. God granted your request in a miraculous way, since you were infertile. As well, God gifted you with the great Mother of God! Surely, you prayed earnestly for your daughter, Mary, during your pregnancy with her in your womb. You must have also prayed during the pregnancy of the Lord Jesus, when he resided in your daughter's womb—his first tabernacle. Please assist me along my own prayer journey awaiting the birth of my grandchild. Pray that I can become more holy throughout this nine-month novena. Please help me to swaddle my unborn grandbaby in loving prayer, together with you, so that he or she will be safe and well, according to God's holy will. Amen.

Cradling with Mama Mary

No doubt, Mama Mary was with you, dear grandma, as you prepared for the birth of your child, whether it was biological or through adoption. Mary loves all of her children and is happy to help us with all family matters. Now, at this time you can wholeheartedly beseech Mama Mary for her loving intercession for your unborn grandchild by praying the "cradling prayer" below each month.

Mama Mary Cradling Prayer

Dear Mother Mary, Mother of Jesus and my Mother, please help me to unite my prayers with yours. My heart is stirred with love, contemplating that our Lord Jesus resided in your holy womb for nine months. You experienced his growth and blessed movements. I can imagine St. Joseph gently placing his weathered hand lovingly on your abdomen to feel your Son's motions and life. Please ask your Son, Jesus, to watch over my unborn grandchild, his or her mother, and me. Please help me to cradle my unborn grandbaby in loving prayer with you and St. Joseph so that my grandchild will be safe and well, according to God's holy will. *Hail Mary*, Amen.

Celebrate your new grandbaby's life all throughout this month. Let each day be enveloped in prayer and thanksgiving. As your heart rejoices, your face will glow with delight in your role as grandmother.

Preparing with the Saints

SAINT JOSEPH

St. Joseph can help us with his powerful intercession. As head of the Holy Family, the humble saint cares about the family. According to Venerable Pope Pius XII, St. Joseph "had to be, because he was married to the Virgin Mary, the purest, the holiest, the most exalted of all God's creatures."[2]

St. Joseph was such an important part of salvation history, yet he was so quiet. Blessed Pope Paul VI said, "The Gospel does not record a single word from him; his language is silence."[3] He was indeed a humble and holy soul.

He was given a spectacular mission to protect his wife, Mary, and their Son, Jesus. After all, their son was none other than the Son of God! Let us turn to St. Joseph, and along with St. Bernardine of Siena cry out: "O Blessed Joseph, be ever mindful of us; give us the benefit of your powerful prayers."

St. Thomas Aquinas has said, "Some saints are privileged to extend to us their patronage with particular efficacy in certain needs, but not in others; but our holy patron St. Joseph has the power to assist us in all cases, in every necessity, in every undertaking."[4] We will discuss St. Joseph in more depth later on. For now, we can focus on the fact that we can turn to him for his powerful intercession in all of our needs, especially those within the family.

Saint Joseph Pregnancy Prayer

Dear St. Joseph, though you remained quiet, you were very heroic and full of God's grace. You were ever attentive to the Holy Spirit and acted upon faith while courageously and lovingly caring for the Holy Family. The saints praise you as a powerful intercessor! St. Teresa of Avila said you never failed to help her. Please look kindly upon my cherished unborn grandchild and beseech our dear Lord to protect his or her precious life, as well as the life of his or her mother. Please help me to grow in holiness throughout this nine-month novena for my grandchild. Amen.

Memorare to Saint Joseph[5]

Remember, most pure spouse of Mary, ever Virgin, my loving protector, St. Joseph, that no one ever had recourse to your protection or asked for your aid without obtaining relief. Confiding, therefore, in your goodness, I come before you and humbly implore you. Despise not my petitions, foster-father of the Redeemer, but graciously receive them. Amen.

Memorare to Mary

Remember, O most gracious Virgin Mary, that never was it known that anyone who fled to thy protection, implored thy help, or sought thine intercession was left unaided. Inspired by this confidence, I fly unto thee, O Virgin of virgins, my mother; to thee do I come, before thee I stand, sinful and sorrowful. O Mother of the Word Incarnate, despise not my petitions, but in thy mercy hear and answer me. Amen.

Prayer to the Holy Family

Lord Jesus Christ, being subject to Mary and Joseph, you sanctified family life by your beautiful virtues. Grant that we, with the help of Mary and Joseph, may be taught by the example of your holy Family, and may after death enjoy its everlasting companionship. Lord Jesus, help us ever to follow the example of your Holy Family, that in the hour of our death your glorious Virgin Mother together with St. Joseph may come to meet us, and we may be worthy to be received by you into the everlasting joys of heaven. You live and reign forever. Amen.

To Ponder in Your Heart

During this first month that your grandchild is in the womb, as you pray for him or her, ponder the words, "Come to me, all you that are weary and are carrying heavy burdens, and I will give you rest" (Matthew 11:28). Take some time to rest in the love of the Lord. Close your eyes and imagine yourself resting against his Sacred Heart. Jesus promises to give rest to your body, heart, and soul!

My reflections on being a Grandparent

THE FIRST MONTH OF PREGNANCY

Giving thanks to God

FOR HAVING CREATED MY GRANDBABY

A prayer in my own words

A Nine-Month Novena

Dear Lord Jesus, Blessed Mother Mary, and all of the angels and saints, please hear my prayer. First, I desire to express my deep gratitude for the blessing of being chosen as a grandmother. I earnestly ask that while I pray for my precious unborn grandchild during this nine-month journey of growth in the womb, that you would watch over me and teach me. I desire to come ever closer to God so that I may become a dazzling example of Christian love to my grandchild—lighting the path to heaven. I pray that the love of God will continually radiate from my heart to touch the hearts of others, especially to all in my family. Thank you, dear Lord, for your abiding love! Amen.

2

Lovingly Praying

"If I had my life to live over, instead of wishing away nine months of pregnancy, I'd have cherished every moment and realized that the wonderment growing inside me was the only chance in life to assist God in a miracle."

—ERMA BOMBECK[6]

Sometimes a mother almost wishes away her pregnancy in a mad rush to get to the finish line. While we can't blame her for her eagerness to hold her sweet baby in her arms, and perhaps, too, to get away from the discomforts that come along with the blessing of life in the womb, we should take the time to pause and ponder all of this. Isn't this particular time in a woman's life remarkable and even miraculous? And, because it is, shouldn't we savor it, as well as do all we can to make it even more sacred, if that be possible? Taking time to ponder the development of precious unborn children while praying for their hidden life in the womb will indeed benefit all of us.

Throughout this second month in the womb, strive to pray many loving prayers of gratitude for your unborn grandchild. And let's now take a look at your grandbaby's progress this month.

Discovering My Grandbaby's Developments

By the end of this month your grandbaby's facial features will begin to develop, and he or she will be between a half-inch and an inch long. Picture the size of a grape. Its heart is beating away, and he or she is quite active, though the movements are not yet felt by mom. Large amounts of red blood cells are moving through its mighty liver. At eight weeks, the beginning of a busy development will commence. Teeth begin to grow under the gums, the intestines will develop, and the facial features will become more developed. The umbilical cord is now noticeable.

My hope and prayer for my grandchild this month
In my own words

Our Example

"Assemble the people for me, and I will let them hear my words,
so that they may learn to fear me as long as they live on the earth,
and may teach their children so."

—Deuteronomy 4:10

In the words above, our Lord mentions that we should fear him. The fear of the Lord is a good thing. It means that we are to respect his authority over us and that we need to obey his laws, which he put into place to assure us of salvation. This important Christian teaching is passed down through the family.

Our teachings, words, and actions—for better or for worse—will be remembered and imitated by future generations. Yes, what we say and do matters very much! That's why, for instance, we don't leave a sharp razor within reach of a small child who has observed his daddy shaving. He wants to be like daddy and might be terribly injured if he tries to shave his tender little face in imitation of his dad.

As your unborn grandchild develops, your prayers will have a positive impact on his or her life. After he or she is born, your teachings will also make a wonderful difference in their life. A grandmother's example is powerful. Keep that in mind as you prayerfully journey through your grandbaby's time in the womb. Later on, your words of wisdom and your virtuous actions will help to pave the way. These are teachings that will become etched upon his or her little heart to be imitated and expressed by them and carried into their own future domestic church.

Be sure to share your personal stories with your grandchild. You might consider writing some of them down in a notebook. At the very least, do not fail in making the time for sharing with your grandchild when the time comes. Your sharing can become a marvelous opportunity to teach Christian values that will counteract the contradictory messages bellowing from today's contemporary culture.

Swaddling with Saint Anne Prayer

Dear St. Anne, mother of the Mother of Jesus, I pray that I may unite my heartfelt prayer to yours and that you will present it before the throne of God. For so long you and Joachim prayed for a child. God granted your request in a miraculous way, since you were infertile. As well, God gifted you with the great Mother of God! Surely, you prayed earnestly for your daughter, Mary, during your pregnancy with her in your womb. You must have also prayed during the pregnancy of the Lord Jesus, when he resided in your daughter's womb—his first tabernacle. Please assist me along my own prayer journey awaiting the birth of my grandchild. Pray that I can become more holy throughout this nine-month novena. Please help me to swaddle my unborn grandbaby in loving prayer, together with you, so that he or she will be safe and well, according to God's holy will. Amen.

Mama Mary Cradling Prayer

Dear Mother Mary, Mother of Jesus and my Mother, please help me to unite my prayers with yours. My heart is stirred with love, contemplating that our Lord Jesus resided in your holy womb for nine months. You experienced his growth and blessed movements. I can imagine St. Joseph gently placing his weathered hand lovingly on your abdomen to feel your Son's motions and life. Please ask your Son, Jesus, to watch over my unborn grandchild, his or her mother, and me. Please help me to cradle my unborn grandbaby in loving prayer with you and St. Joseph so that my grandchild will be safe and well, according to God's holy will. *Hail Mary,* Amen.

Just What the Doctor Ordered

As your sweet grandbaby grows within its mother's womb, your heart leaps with joy over the blessing that God has bestowed upon you—the amazing vocation of being a grandmother! Relish in that sweet joy this month.

Preparing with the Saints

ZÉLIE AND LOUIS MARTIN

St. Zélie Guérin Martin was never a grandmother because all of her children would enter religious life. On October 18, 2015, Pope Francis canonized her along with her husband, Louis Martin; they were the first ever married couple with children to be canonized in the same ceremony. Pope Francis said at their canonization, "The holy spouses Louis Martin and Marie-Azelie Guerin practiced Christian service in the family, creating day by day an environment of faith and love which nurtured the vocations of their daughters, among whom was Saint Therese of the Child Jesus."[7]

Before they met, both Louis and Zélie initially thought they each had vocations in the Church as vowed religious. However, they were each turned down; Louis was turned down for failing Latin, and Zélie was turned away by the sisters of the Hotel-Dieu for reasons not known.

This holy couple would later meet in Alençon and would marry on July 13, 1858. They brought nine children into the world, and Zélie would express her happiness over such a family. "We lived only for them," Zélie stated. "They were all our happiness." Yet, in God's mysterious providence, within a few years' time Zélie and Louis lost four of their small children to illness. They could barely stand the sorrow, and some told Zélie she would have been better off had they never been born. Those comments, though possibly well-meaning, felt as if a sword were thrust through her heart. Zélie knew all about eternal life and expressed it in a letter she wrote to her sister: "My children were not lost forever; life is short and full of miseries, and we shall find our little ones again up above."

Still, sorrow filled her motherly heart, and she continued on each day the best she could. She expressed, "I haven't a penny's worth of courage." But still she walked forward in faith. By God's grace, she and Louis brought another baby into the world. This baby, along with their other four living daughters (Marie,

Pauline, Léonie, and Céline), would later enter religious life. This last baby, whom they named Marie-Françoise-Thérèse, would later become known as St. Thérèse of Lisieux. She would be known far and wide as the "Little Flower" and would become a Doctor of the Church. Can we even imagine having all of our children or our grandchildren enter religious life? On top of that, both parents became canonized saints!

Take some time to ponder your role in your family's life. Are there steps that you can take to grow in holiness? Could you carve out additional quiet time to spend with Jesus and his holy Mother Mary each day? Now, offer to God your heartfelt prayer for your unborn grandchild.

Saint Joseph Pregnancy Prayer

Dear St. Joseph, though you remained quiet, you were very heroic and full of God's grace. You were ever attentive to the Holy Spirit and acted upon faith while courageously and lovingly caring for the Holy Family. The saints praise you as a powerful intercessor! St. Teresa of Avila said you never failed to help her. Please look kindly upon my cherished unborn grandchild and beseech our dear Lord to protect his or her precious life, as well as the life of his or her mother. Please help me to grow in holiness throughout this nine-month novena for my grandchild. Amen.

Memorare to Saint Joseph[8]

Remember, most pure spouse of Mary, ever Virgin, my loving protector, St. Joseph, that no one ever had recourse to your protection or asked for your aid without obtaining relief. Confiding, therefore, in your goodness, I come before you and humbly implore you. Despise not my petitions, foster-father of the Redeemer, but graciously receive them. Amen.

Memorare to Mary

Remember, O most gracious Virgin Mary, that never was it known that anyone who fled to thy protection, implored thy help, or sought thine intercession was left unaided. Inspired by this confidence, I fly unto thee, O Virgin of virgins, my mother; to thee do I come, before thee I stand, sinful and sorrowful. O Mother of the Word Incarnate, despise not my petitions, but in thy mercy hear and answer me. Amen.

Prayer to the Holy Family

Lord Jesus Christ, being subject to Mary and Joseph, you sanctified family life by your beautiful virtues. Grant that we, with the help of Mary and Joseph, may be taught by the example of your holy Family, and may after death enjoy its everlasting companionship. Lord Jesus, help us ever to follow the example of your Holy Family, that in the hour of our death your glorious Virgin Mother together with St. Joseph may come to meet us, and we may be worthy to be received by you into the everlasting joys of heaven. You live and reign forever. Amen.

To Ponder in Your Heart

During this second month of your grandchild's development, take a moment to ponder these beautiful words: "Grandchildren are the crown of the aged, and the glory of children is their parents" (Proverbs 17:6). Spend time in thankful prayer this month, praising God for the great gift of your grandchild—an unrepeatable and unique life. Your grandchild was destined from all eternity! Think about that.

My reflections on being a grandparent
THE SECOND MONTH OF PREGNANCY

_____

_____

_____

_____

_____

_____

_____

_____

Giving thanks to God for creating my grandbaby
A prayer in my own words

_____

_____

_____

_____

_____

_____

A Nine-Month Novena

To pray each day throughout this month

Dear Lord Jesus, Blessed Mother Mary, and all of the angels and saints, please hear my prayer. First, I desire to express my deep gratitude for the blessing of being chosen as a grandmother. I earnestly ask that while I pray for my precious unborn grandchild during this nine-month journey of growth in the womb, that you would watch over me and teach me. I desire to come ever closer to God so that I may become a dazzling example of Christian love to my grandchild—lighting the path to heaven. I pray that the love of God will continually radiate from my heart to touch the hearts of others, especially to all in my family. Thank you, dear Lord, for your abiding love! Amen.

Praying with Hope

*For this child I prayed; and the LORD has granted me the petition
that I made to him. Therefore I have lent him to the LORD;
as long as he lives, he is given to the LORD."*

—1 SAMUEL 1:27–28

Children are a great gift from God. There is no doubt about that. Yet, sometimes people believe that having children or grandchildren is their "right." It's not. And there are some who feel that they can dispose of the unborn child when it is not convenient for them or for some other reason. This is altogether tragic. We must continue to pray for these individuals, as well as for a greater awareness of the eminent sanctity of all human life. Every single baby conceived is a unique and individual human being who needs only time and nutrition in order to survive outside the womb. Every single baby deserves to be loved and have the chance to give love someday.

God gifts children to us, and we are grateful and filled with joy. Yet, we must also trust God when he takes them away. I sincerely know that this might not be a happy thought, especially because I have lost three babies to miscarriage. But as much as we might wish that God would not allow the loss of unborn babies to miscarriage, it is a reality. Oftentimes, God's ways are mysterious to us. We can trust that all babies are safe with him in heaven.

In the verse that begins this chapter we read that we should lend children to the Lord. Truth be told, children are actually on loan to us! Let us trust God that he knows what is best and let us also accept his marvelous loving gifts of life that he sends to us.

Now is a good time to pray for the families who have lost babies.

Compassionate God, soothe the hearts of [insert the parents' names here], and grant that through the prayers of Mary, who grieved by the Cross of her Son, you may enlighten their faith, give hope to their hearts, and peace to their lives. Lord, grant mercy to all the members of this family and comfort them with the hope that one day we will all live with you, with your Son Jesus Christ, and the Holy Spirit, forever and ever. Amen.[9]

Throughout this third month in the womb, strive to pray many loving prayers of hope for your unborn grandchild. And let's take a look at your grandbaby's progress thus far.

Discovering My Grandbaby's Developments

Your precious unborn grandchild has been continuously growing, and by the end of the month he or she will be already about two inches (or a bit more) in size (from crown to rump). Your grandchild is about an ounce in weight, the head being the largest part of the body, and it has become rounder and more developed. He or she has eyes, a nose, a forehead, a little chin, and teeth that are partially formed under the gums. Petite fingers and toes are almost completely formed, and fingernails are sprouting. Reflexes are functioning. Major organs are being developed from its stem cells (brain, heart, liver, bone, immune system, and nerve cells). The digestive tract is now functioning.

My hope and prayer for my grandchild this month
In my own words

SAINT ANNE, SAINT JOACHIM, AND MARY

St. Anne and St. Joachim were chosen by God to be the parents of the Blessed Mother who would give birth to Jesus Christ. This, of course, made Anne and Joachim the immediate grandparents of Jesus. But let's step back a bit to see exactly how this miracle mystically unfolded.

Anne and Joachim were devout Jews who ardently prayed for the coming of the Messiah. Before meeting one another, they each had prayed that they could find and wed a holy spouse. By God's amazing and mysterious providence, their prayers were presented to the throne of God at the same time. Subsequently, they were each visited by the Angel Gabriel—to Anne in person and to Joachim in a dream—with the message that their prayers would be answered and they should wed. They married and led virtuous and very happy wedded lives. However, Anne was found to be infertile, and this caused much reproach and insults from neighbors. Twenty years later they were still childless.

It was apparent that God was asking the holy couple for patience, and so they continued to offer prayers of petition for a child as they also kept up their prayers for the coming of the Messiah. They promised God that if they were blessed with a child they would consecrate him or her to God's service in the Temple of Jerusalem. One time when Joachim was in the Temple praying for these things, a priest rebuked him and told him to leave; the priest said that Joachim was not pleasing to God since he was childless. Joachim humbly prayed some more and left, hanging his head in sorrow, accepting God's will for him and his wife—whatever that might be. He immediately went off to his farm where for days in solitude he poured his heart out to God. He begged the Lord to be good to Anne even if he himself wasn't worthy of a child.

In God's great love and mercy, Anne and Joachim's patience and perseverance would be rewarded in ways they could never have imagined. Deep in contemplative prayer and wrapped in the mystery of the Incarnation, Anne suddenly received a visit from the Angel Gabriel, who came to let her know that her prayers were pleasing to the Almighty. The Angel also visited Joachim in his solitude. According to the Venerable Mother Mary of Jesus of Agreda, a mystic, also known as the Blue Nun (1602–1665), the Holy Trinity instructed the Angel Gabriel to tell Anne and Joachim that their prayers had been heard. Specifically, Gabriel was told, "Promise them that by the favor of our right Hand they will receive the Fruit of benediction, and that Anne shall conceive a daughter to Whom We give the name Mary."[10]

The baby's conception would be miraculous since Anne was infertile. We can only imagine the impact of this news. The Holy Spirit was right there, as well, to support Anne while she was listening to the message, or else she might have fainted away in sheer joy. Anne was also enlightened by the angel that it was not just *any* baby she would be given, but she would nurture and give birth to the mother of the Messiah! She had to keep that earth-shattering excitement quiet and safe within her heart. She was not to tell Joachim or anyone else. However, later, in Joachim's last days, God would reveal the great privilege to him.

Anne and Joachim were told by the Angel Gabriel to continue to pray and lead holy lives. So they prayed and waited. And at the appointed time the Blessed Virgin Mary was conceived in Anne's womb. The holy parents went straight to the temple in Jerusalem to give thanks to God. They made a promise together that day to offer their daughter to God's service in the temple, and that each year on the same day they would return there for a day of praise and thanksgiving, offering gifts and alms. They kept this vow until their deaths.

Swaddling with Saint Anne Prayer

Dear St. Anne, mother of the Mother of Jesus, I pray that I may unite my heartfelt prayer to yours and that you will present it before the throne of God. For so long you and Joachim prayed for a child. God granted your request in a miraculous way, since you were infertile. As well, God gifted you with the great Mother of God! Surely, you prayed earnestly for your daughter, Mary, during your pregnancy with her in your womb. You must have also prayed during the pregnancy of the Lord Jesus, when he resided in your daughter's womb—his first tabernacle. Please assist me along my own prayer journey awaiting the birth of my grandchild. Pray that I can become more holy throughout this nine-month novena. Please help me to swaddle my unborn grandbaby in loving prayer, together with you, so that he or she will be safe and well, according to God's holy will. Amen.

Mama Mary Cradling Prayer

Dear Mother Mary, Mother of Jesus and my Mother, please help me to unite my prayers with yours. My heart is stirred with love, contemplating that our Lord Jesus resided in your holy womb for nine months. You experienced his growth and blessed movements. I can imagine St. Joseph gently placing his weathered hand lovingly on your abdomen to feel your Son's motions and life. Please ask your Son, Jesus, to watch over my unborn grandchild, his or her mother, and me. Please help me to cradle my unborn grandbaby in loving prayer with you and St. Joseph so that my grandchild will be safe and well, according to God's holy will. *Hail Mary,* Amen.

Just What the Doctor Ordered

Your unborn grandchild is on a beautiful and prayerful journey. Technically, only time and nutrition are needed before he or she, Lord willing, sees the light of day. I would like to add that prayer and love are essential elements as well! Enjoy this month of growth and blessing.

Preparing with the Saints

ANNE AND JOACHIM

What can we learn from St. Anne and St. Joachim? First of all, consider that they were faithful to God in all things. Before knowing one another, they prayed for one another, desiring a holy spouse. Then, together in marriage, they prayed to be blessed with a child. Day in and day out they prayed. Twenty years later, there was no child to hold, to kiss, to care for. Did they give up praying? No, they persevered.

They were ridiculed and rebuked because the townspeople and neighbors saw their lack of children as a curse or punishment from God. Yet, Anne and Joachim continued to trust in God's holy will. And in his perfect timing, God indeed answered their prayers. He blessed them in a manner much more incredible than they could have thought to request. In fact, the Holy Spirit supported Anne when the Angel Gabriel told her the news that her child was to be the Mother of God! We can only attempt to imagine those amazing, miraculous moments when heaven touched earth and pierced human hearts.

When it was time for Mary's birth at twelve in the evening, one thousand angels were all around. In fact, the angels had been assigned long before that amazing moment. They were there to protect Anne and the unborn Mary all throughout the birth. When Mary arrived, Anne wrapped her little baby in swaddling clothes. She immediately offered her infant to God through tears of joy.

"Lord of infinite wisdom and power, Creator of all that exists," she said, "this Fruit of my womb which I have received of Thy bounty, I offer to Thee with eternal thanks, for without any merit of mine Thou hast vouchsafed it to me." Anne continued, "Dispose Thou of the mother and Child according to thy most holy Will and look propitiously down upon our lowliness from thy exalted throne. Be Thou eternally blessed, because Thou hast enriched the world with a Creature so pleasing to thy bounty and because in her Thou hast prepared a dwelling-place and a tabernacle for the eternal Word. . . . Give me, O my Lord and King, the necessary enlightenment to know thy Will and to execute it according to thy pleasure in the service of my Daughter."[11]

Saint Joseph Pregnancy Prayer

Dear St. Joseph, though you remained quiet, you were very heroic and full of God's grace. You were ever attentive to the Holy Spirit and acted upon faith while courageously and lovingly caring for the Holy Family. The saints praise you as a powerful intercessor! St. Teresa of Avila said you never failed to help her. Please look kindly upon my cherished unborn grandchild and beseech our dear Lord to protect his or her precious life, as well as the life of his or her mother. Please help me to grow in holiness throughout this nine-month novena for my grandchild. Amen.

Memorare to Saint Joseph[12]

Remember, most pure spouse of Mary, ever Virgin, my loving protector, St. Joseph, that no one ever had recourse to your protection or asked for your aid without obtaining relief. Confiding, therefore, in your goodness, I come before you and humbly implore you. Despise not my petitions, foster-father of the Redeemer, but graciously receive them. Amen.

Memorare to Mary

Remember, O most gracious Virgin Mary, that never was it known that anyone who fled to thy protection, implored thy help, or sought thine intercession was left unaided. Inspired by this confidence, I fly unto thee, O Virgin of virgins, my mother; to thee do I come, before thee I stand, sinful and sorrowful. O Mother of the Word Incarnate, despise not my petitions, but in thy mercy hear and answer me. Amen.

Prayer to the Holy Family

Lord Jesus Christ, being subject to Mary and Joseph, you sanctified family life by your beautiful virtues. Grant that we, with the help of Mary and Joseph, may be taught by the example of your holy Family, and may after death enjoy its everlasting companionship. Lord Jesus, help us ever to follow the example of your Holy Family, that in the hour of our death your glorious Virgin Mother together with St. Joseph may come to meet us, and we may be worthy to be received by you into the everlasting joys of heaven. You live and reign forever. Amen.

To Ponder in Your Heart

Our Lord works miracles in our hearts and lives. He asks for our perseverance in prayer and our trust in him. During this third month of your grandchild's development, try to pray often, "Jesus, I trust in You." It's not always easy to trust Jesus, but he is very pleased when we do. Also, making an act of trust such as this helps to change things. We trust and we move forward in faith.

My reflections on being a Grandparent
THE THIRD MONTH OF PREGNANCY

Giving thanks to God for having created my grandbaby
A prayer in my own words

_____

_____

_____

_____

_____

_____

_____

_____

A Nine-Month Novena
To pray each day throughout this month

Dear Lord Jesus, Blessed Mother Mary, and all of the angels and saints, please hear my prayer. First, I desire to express my deep gratitude for the blessing of being chosen as a grandmother. I earnestly ask that while I pray for my precious unborn grandchild during this nine-month journey of growth in the womb, that you would watch over me and teach me. I desire to come ever closer to God so that I may become a dazzling example of Christian love to my grandchild—lighting the path to heaven. I pray that the love of God will continually radiate from my heart to touch the hearts of others, especially to all in my family. Thank you, dear Lord, for your abiding love! Amen.

Joyfully Praying

For surely I know the plans I have for you, says the LORD, plans for your welfare and not for harm, to give you a future with hope.
—JEREMIAH 29:11

It's possible that you have pondered your grandchild's future, even just a bit. You might have envisioned him or her in your arms, up close to your joyful heart. Certainly, holding and nestling our grandchildren is one of the best blessings ever! We can never "spoil" our grandchild with love.

You might have pictured your little toddler grandchild playing with you, romping around, singing—even learning to pray as you teach him or her to make the Sign of the Cross and offer to God simple heartfelt words of gratitude.

As well, your heart might hold prayerful and earnest hopes for a bright future for your grandchild as he or she grows up within the blessedness of the family to one day launch out on their own. Grandparents pray fervently that the spiritual foundation which they have helped to build within the heart of their grandchild, will withstand every storm that the future holds.

The words above from Jeremiah tell us that the Lord surely knows the plans that he has for each one of us. We must trust God with our lives, as well as with our grandchildren's lives. We should be confident that our prayers do make a difference and will indeed be a powerful influence in the lives of our grandchildren.

Throughout this fourth month in the womb, strive to pray many joyful prayers of gratitude for your unborn grandchild. Let's take a look at your grandbaby's progress thus far.

Discovering My Grandbaby's Developments

During this month in the womb, your grandchild's heartbeat may become audible and detected by an instrument called a Doppler. The reproductive organs and genitalia are now fully developed, and if an ultrasound is conducted this month, the technician or doctor may be able to detect if it is a girl or a boy. An ultrasound is usually conducted at around 18 to 20 weeks. So, this may happen next month.

The nervous system is beginning to function. His or her teeth and bones become denser and fingers and toes are now fully formed. He or she has eyelids, eyelashes, hair, and nails. He or she can even suck on their thumb, and this is sometimes caught on ultrasound! He or she can also make faces, yawn, and stretch. The baby can hear your voice! Speak to him or her often, as well as encourage mom and dad to speak and sing to their unborn child.

My hope and prayer for my grandchild this month
In my own words

Holy Insights

THE VISITATION

Immediately after Mary of Nazareth was greeted by the Angel Gabriel at the Annunciation, she headed for the hill country, where she would enter the house of Zachariah and greet her cousin Elizabeth. The Gospel of Luke tells us, "Mary set out and went with haste" (Luke 1:39). What was Mary's rush?

First, let's take a quick look at the journey. In many ways the journey was a rough one because the terrain was rugged and Mary's mode of transportation was a donkey. Remember, it was "hill country," otherwise known as the Judean mountains. It was a ninety- or one hundred-mile trek from Nazareth to the Judean hill country. Yet, Mary put her own comforts aside—which might have included the shock she could have felt to become suddenly entrusted with one of the greatest missions ever—to nurture the Son of God in her own womb and in nine months to give birth to him! She might have also been experiencing some early pregnancy discomforts.

Mary felt compelled to get straightaway to her older cousin's home, where she could help since Elizabeth was getting on in age. As well, Mary must have been eager to share her joyful news with Elizabeth. Mary knew what she needed to do and didn't waste time. The Angel Gabriel had told Mary, "And now, your relative Elizabeth in her old age has also conceived a son; and this is the sixth month for her who was said to be barren. For nothing will be impossible with God" (Luke 1:36–37). So, after she addressed the angel, giving her wondrous *fiat* to God— "Here am I, the servant of the Lord; let it be with me according to your word"—off she went!

What can you learn from Mary's generous servant heart? Do you have a heart that desires to serve? How can you emulate her virtues? Take some time today and this month to ponder this.

Now, offer to God your heartfelt prayer for your unborn grandchild.

Swaddling with Saint Anne Prayer

Dear St. Anne, mother of the Mother of Jesus, I pray that I may unite my heartfelt prayer to yours and that you will present it before the throne of God. For so long you and Joachim prayed for a child. God granted your request in a miraculous way, since you were infertile. As well, God gifted you with the great Mother of God! Surely, you prayed earnestly for your daughter, Mary, during your pregnancy with her in your womb. You must have also prayed during the pregnancy of the Lord Jesus, when he resided in your daughter's womb—his first tabernacle. Please assist me along my own prayer journey awaiting the birth of my grandchild. Pray that I can become more holy throughout this nine-month novena. Please help me to swaddle my unborn grandbaby in loving prayer, together with you, so that he or she will be safe and well, according to God's holy will. Amen.

Mama Mary Cradling Prayer

Dear Mother Mary, Mother of Jesus and my Mother, please help me to unite my prayers with yours. My heart is stirred with love, contemplating that our Lord Jesus resided in your holy womb for nine months. You experienced his growth and blessed movements. I can imagine St. Joseph gently placing his weathered hand lovingly on your abdomen to feel your Son's motions and life. Please ask your Son, Jesus, to watch over my unborn grandchild, his or her mother, and me. Please help me to cradle my unborn grandbaby in loving prayer with you and St. Joseph so that my grandchild will be safe and well, according to God's holy will. *Hail Mary,* Amen.

Just What the Doctor Ordered

Your role as a grandmother might seem a bit hidden right now as you offer heartfelt quiet prayers for your unborn grandbaby. Nonetheless, yours is a most particular and exceptional role. A grandmother's love is like no other. Enjoy this month of prayer and pondering.

Preparing with the Saints

ELIZABETH AND ZACHARIAH

St. Elizabeth was married to St. Zachariah. They were a childless couple who diligently followed God's commandments and ordinances. One time when Zachariah was in the Temple, the Angel Gabriel visited him and delivered an answer to prayer in the form of an extraordinary promise that was very difficult for Zachariah to comprehend and believe.

The angel first quieted Zachariah's fears and then explained what was about to happen. "Do not be afraid, Zechariah, for your prayer has been heard. Your wife Elizabeth will bear you a son, and you will name him John." We can imagine Zachariah's perplexed thoughts at that moment. But he no doubt listened intently to the captivating words from the radiant being.

The angel continued, "You will have joy and gladness, and many will rejoice at his birth, for he will be great in the sight of the Lord. He must never drink wine or strong drink; even before his birth he will be filled with the Holy Spirit" (Luke 1:13–15). But, even though the angel gave these amazing prophesies, this miraculous visit and these astonishing words seemed much too good to be true to Zachariah. He asked, "How can I be sure of this? I am an old man and my wife is well along in years."

"I am Gabriel. I stand in the presence of God, and I have been sent to speak to you and to tell you this good news." Zachariah still had a hard time believing—and there would be a consequence to Zachariah's disbelief. The angel said, "But now, because you did not believe my words, which will be fulfilled in their time, you will become mute, unable to speak, until the day these things occur" (Luke 1:16–23).

Zachariah was in the Temple for some time and people wondered why. But when he came out, he could not speak to them. Instead, he made hand motions, and the people surmised that he must have seen a vision.

Later, when Zachariah's wife, Elizabeth, conceived a baby as predicted and the baby was to be known as John the Baptist, Zachariah received his voice back. Elizabeth and Zachariah's earnest prayer for a child was answered in a miraculous way, a way that they never would have imagined. And not just *any* child was given to them, but John the Baptist! John would prepare the way for Jesus.

Take some time to ponder God's generosity. Sit quietly, close your eyes, and imagine yourself in the scene when John the Baptist was born. You too can give praise to God!

Saint Joseph Pregnancy Prayer

Dear St. Joseph, though you remained quiet, you were very heroic and full of God's grace. You were ever attentive to the Holy Spirit and acted upon faith while courageously and lovingly caring for the Holy Family. The saints praise you as a powerful intercessor! St. Teresa of Avila said you never failed to help her. Please look kindly upon my cherished unborn grandchild and beseech our dear Lord to protect his or her precious life, as well as the life of his or her mother. Please help me to grow in holiness throughout this nine-month novena for my grandchild. Amen.

Memorare to Saint Joseph[13]

Remember, most pure spouse of Mary, ever Virgin, my loving protector, St. Joseph, that no one ever had recourse to your protection or asked for your aid without obtaining relief. Confiding, therefore, in your goodness, I come before you and humbly implore you. Despise not my petitions, foster-father of the Redeemer, but graciously receive them. Amen.

Memorare to Mary

Remember, O most gracious Virgin Mary, that never was it known that anyone who fled to thy protection, implored thy help, or sought thine intercession was left unaided. Inspired by this confidence, I fly unto thee, O Virgin of virgins, my mother; to thee do I come, before thee I stand, sinful and sorrowful. O Mother of the Word Incarnate, despise not my petitions, but in thy mercy hear and answer me. Amen.

Prayer to the Holy Family

Lord Jesus Christ, being subject to Mary and Joseph, you sanctified family life by your beautiful virtues. Grant that we, with the help of Mary and Joseph, may be taught by the example of your holy Family, and may after death enjoy its everlasting companionship. Lord Jesus, help us ever to follow the example of your Holy Family, that in the hour of our death your glorious Virgin Mother together with St. Joseph may come to meet us, and we may be worthy to be received by you into the everlasting joys of heaven. You live and reign forever. Amen.

To Ponder in Your Heart

During this fourth month of your grandchild's development, take time to ponder St. Elizabeth's words to her cousin Mary: "Blessed are you among women, and blessed is the fruit of your womb." Close your eyes and imagine yourself in the scene of the Visitation as you also express these words to the Blessed Mother. These are words that we can say to Mary every single day. Hopefully, we are praying this special statement many times a day as we voice our Hail Marys and pray our Rosaries.

My reflections on being a Grandparent
The fourth month of pregnancy

Giving thanks to God for having created my grandbaby

A prayer in my own words

_____

_____

_____

_____

_____

_____

_____

_____

_____

A Nine-Month Novena

To pray each day throughout this month

Dear Lord Jesus, Blessed Mother Mary, and all of the angels and saints, please hear my prayer. First, I desire to express my deep gratitude for the blessing of being chosen as a grandmother. I earnestly ask that while I pray for my precious unborn grandchild during this nine-month journey of growth in the womb, that you would watch over me and teach me. I desire to come ever closer to God so that I may become a dazzling example of Christian love to my grandchild—lighting the path to heaven. I pray that the love of God will continually radiate from my heart to touch the hearts of others, especially to all in my family. Thank you, dear Lord, for your abiding love! Amen.

5

Perseveringly Praying

Do not worry about anything, but in everything by prayer and supplication
with thanksgiving let your requests be made known to God.
And the peace of God, which surpasses all understanding, will guard your
hearts and your minds in Christ Jesus.
—PHILIPPIANS 4:6–7

Our chapter title suggests we should pray perseveringly. As well, our verse this month tells us not to worry about anything but to pray, petition, and thank Our Lord. Perseverance in prayer might seem a bit daunting. After all, life is busy in the family, and we are often distracted by a myriad of responsibilities and activities. Yet, as Christians, we are urged, "Rejoice always, pray without ceasing, give thanks in all circumstances; for this is the will of God in Christ Jesus for you" (1 Thessalonians 5:16–18).

Let's take that apart—one directive at a time. 1) We should rejoice always. Rejoicing can be difficult in challenging times, yet we can pray for God's graces to be a more rejoicing sort of soul. 2) We are to pray without ceasing. This means that our lives are to be prayerful. We can form prayer habits for praying throughout the day. As well, we can pray that our life can become a beautiful prayer to God because of our lives of Christian love. 3) We are to give thanks in all circumstances. Certainly, that should not be difficult to do, being the grandmother of an unborn grandchild! But also, we should give thanks through the nitty-gritty details of life—the contradictions and pinpricks that we can offer up in a prayer of thanks to God for allowing us an opportunity to pray for the one who is persecuting us, or the one who misunderstands our Christianity.

As well, we experience loss, and we can be sorrowful. Yet, we can still try to "rejoice always" by offering our sorrow or pain to God and ask him to help us rejoice. We know that there is something much better than our lives here on earth. We can look forward to Eternal Life! That alone can help us to sincerely rejoice.

There are endless reasons to rejoice, pray without ceasing, and give thanks. Let's hang on to the last line in our verse above: "And the peace of God, which surpasses all understanding, will guard your hearts and your minds in Christ Jesus." May God's peace enter our hearts and souls. Throughout this fifth month in the womb, strive to pray perseveringly.

Let's take a look at your grandbaby's progress thus far.

Discovering My Grandbaby's Developments

Your unborn grandchild's overall size is about that of an avocado. The legs are more developed and the soft cartilage is hardening into bone. The umbilical cord is stronger and thicker, and your grandchild has begun to flex his or her legs. Mom might be able to feel this. The senses of smell, sight, touch, taste, and hearing are developing. By the end of this month he or she will be able to swallow, will be about halfway through the pregnancy, will be about six and a half inches from head to rump, and will weigh about 11 ounces.

My hope and prayer for my grandchild this month
In my own words

_____

_____

_____

_____

_____

Holy Insights

We discussed Mary and Elizabeth's beautiful Visitation earlier. Let's delve a bit deeper.

God sent the Angel Gabriel to Mary not only to tell her that he had chosen her to be the Mother of God, but also to inform her that her cousin Elizabeth, who had previously been barren, had conceived a child. God's graces filled Mary's heart with charity, and with Jesus residing within her womb, she set out to visit her elderly cousin Elizabeth so that she could assist her. Perhaps she even knew or sensed that there was a special relationship between Elizabeth's child and her own.

Elizabeth had been ridiculed by many who viewed Elizabeth's inability to conceive as a punishment from God. When Elizabeth was gifted with her miraculous pregnancy of John the Baptist, she withdrew for five months, no doubt in prayer and in thanksgiving. Scripture tells us, "After those days his wife Elizabeth conceived, and for five months she remained in seclusion. She said, 'This is what the Lord has done for me when he looked favorably on me and took away the disgrace I have endured among my people'" (Luke 1:24–25).

When Mary finally arrived at Elizabeth's home after her long hundred-mile journey, she greeted Elizabeth with a warm embrace. No doubt, along with Mary, God's grace entered the house. We learn from Scripture, "When Elizabeth heard Mary's greeting, the child leaped in her womb. And Elizabeth was filled with the Holy Spirit" (Luke 1:41). Sanctified by the presence of Jesus, John the Baptist reacted!

Magnificent graces were unfolding, and the Holy Spirit was powerfully working. St. Elizabeth heartily exclaimed, "Blessed are you among women, and blessed is the fruit of your womb. And why has this happened to me, that the mother of my Lord comes to me? For as soon as I heard the sound of your greeting, the child in my womb leaped for joy. And blessed is she who believed that there would be a fulfillment of what was spoken to her by the Lord" (Luke 1:42–45).

Mary didn't go to Elizabeth's home to be praised. Though she knew that Elizabeth was correct about the fact that she was indeed the mother of the Lord, and though filled with grace, she was also filled with great humility. Mary chose to speak of her own "lowliness" and would give glory and praise to God. She answered her cousin Elizabeth with her marvelous song of praise, which is what we now call the Canticle of Mary or the Magnificat:

My soul magnifies the Lord,
    and my spirit rejoices in God my Savior,
for he has looked with favor on the lowliness of his servant.
    Surely, from now on all generations will call me blessed;
for the Mighty One has done great things for me,
    and holy is his name.
His mercy is for those who fear him
    from generation to generation.
He has shown strength with his arm;
    he has scattered the proud in the thoughts of their hearts.
He has brought down the powerful from their thrones,
    and lifted up the lowly;
he has filled the hungry with good things,
    and sent the rich away empty.
He has helped his servant Israel,
    in remembrance of his mercy,
according to the promise he made to our ancestors,
    to Abraham and to his descendants forever.
        (Luke 1:46–55)

Take some time to ponder the entire scene between Elizabeth and Mary—between the unborn John the Baptist and the unborn Jesus. Certainly, God desires that we would all be transformed by the presence of Jesus and Mary. Meditate on Mary's beautiful words—her song of praise. Strive to pray this prayer each day this month as you actively pray for your unborn grandbaby.

Now, offer to God your heartfelt prayers for your unborn grandchild. No doubt you will pray perseveringly this month for your precious little one.

Swaddling with Saint Anne Prayer

Dear St. Anne, mother of the Mother of Jesus, I pray that I may unite my heartfelt prayer to yours and that you will present it before the throne of God. For so long you and Joachim prayed for a child. God granted your request in a miraculous way, since you were infertile. As well, God gifted you with the great Mother of God! Surely, you prayed earnestly for your daughter, Mary, during your pregnancy with her in your womb. You must have also prayed during the pregnancy of the Lord Jesus, when he resided in your daughter's womb—his first tabernacle. Please assist me along my own prayer journey awaiting the birth of my grandchild. Pray that I can become more holy throughout this nine-month novena. Please help me to swaddle my unborn grandbaby in loving prayer, together with you, so that he or she will be safe and well, according to God's holy will. Amen.

Mama Mary Cradling Prayer

Dear Mother Mary, Mother of Jesus and my Mother, please help me to unite my prayers with yours. My heart is stirred with love, contemplating that our Lord Jesus resided in your holy womb for nine months. You experienced his growth and blessed movements. I can imagine St. Joseph gently placing his weathered hand lovingly on your abdomen to feel your Son's motions and life. Please ask your Son, Jesus, to watch over my unborn grandchild, his or her mother, and me. Please help me to cradle my unborn grandbaby in loving prayer with you and St. Joseph so that my grandchild will be safe and well, according to God's holy will. *Hail Mary,* Amen.

Just What the Doctor Ordered

How wonderful it is to be a Christian grandmother and able to ponder such wonderful things. Our faith is rich and inexhaustible! Throughout this month, take time to meditate upon the unfathomable miracle of human life.

Preparing with the Saints

SAINT TERESA OF CALCUTTA

St. Teresa of Calcutta often spoke about the Visitation of Mary and Elizabeth. She emphasized that Mary was a humble handmaid and missionary. Specifically, she said, "Mary was a true missionary because she was not afraid to be the handmaid of the Lord. She went in haste to put her beautiful humility into a living action of love, to do the handmaid's work for Elizabeth."

Mother Teresa added, "We know what this humility obtained for the unborn child: he 'leapt with joy' in the womb of his mother—the first human being to recognize the coming of Christ; and then the mother of the Lord sang with joy, with gratitude, and praise."[14]

Mother Teresa also stated, "Mary had a call and a mission, and she went through a process of discernment to accept them." She explained that Mary did ask a question of the angel. Mary asked, "How can this be since I am a virgin?" (Luke 1:34). After the angel made clear to Mary, "The Holy Spirit will come upon you, and the power of the Most High will overshadow you; therefore the child to be born will be holy; he will be called Son of God" (Luke 1:35), Mother Teresa explained, "Mary then responded to the angel in obedience and rejoiced, saying, 'yes,'" then added, "All mankind rejoices with her in her 'yes.' She had been chosen as the Queen of Heaven and Earth, yet she did not go in search of glory or even to tell Joseph."[15]

Mother Teresa modeled herself after the Blessed Virgin Mary and encouraged and taught her sisters in religious life to do so, as well. You can ask Mary to intercede for you and your unborn grandchild. Pause and pray earnestly to the Blessed Mother this month, asking her to grant many graces to you.

Saint Joseph Pregnancy Prayer

Dear St. Joseph, though you remained quiet, you were very heroic and full of God's grace. You were ever attentive to the Holy Spirit and acted upon faith while courageously and lovingly caring for the Holy Family. The saints praise you as a powerful intercessor! St. Teresa of Avila said you never failed to help her. Please look kindly upon my cherished unborn grandchild and beseech our dear Lord to protect his or her precious life, as well as the life of his or her mother. Please help me to grow in holiness throughout this nine-month novena for my grandchild. Amen.

Memorare to Saint Joseph[16]

Remember, most pure spouse of Mary, ever Virgin, my loving protector, St. Joseph, that no one ever had recourse to your protection or asked for your aid without obtaining relief. Confiding, therefore, in your goodness, I come before you and humbly implore you. Despise not my petitions, foster-father of the Redeemer, but graciously receive them. Amen.

Memorare to Mary

Remember, O most gracious Virgin Mary, that never was it known that anyone who fled to thy protection, implored thy help, or sought thine intercession was left unaided. Inspired by this confidence, I fly unto thee, O Virgin of virgins, my mother; to thee do I come, before thee I stand, sinful and sorrowful. O Mother of the Word Incarnate, despise not my petitions, but in thy mercy hear and answer me. Amen.

Prayer to the Holy Family

Lord Jesus Christ, being subject to Mary and Joseph, you sanctified family life by your beautiful virtues. Grant that we, with the help of Mary and Joseph, may be taught by the example of your holy Family, and may after death enjoy its everlasting companionship. Lord Jesus, help us ever to follow the example of your Holy Family, that in the hour of our death your glorious Virgin Mother together with St. Joseph may come to meet us, and we may be worthy to be received by you into the everlasting joys of heaven. You live and reign forever. Amen.

To Ponder in Your Heart

During this fifth month of your grandchild's development, ponder the Blessed Virgin Mary's words in her song of praise. "My soul magnifies the Lord, and my spirit rejoices in God my Savior, for he has looked with favor on the lowliness of his servant." How might you emulate her humility? Ask Mary to help you—day by day.

As well, strive to hand over all of your worries to the Lord. Throughout this month, take time to ponder these words from Philippians 4:7: "And the peace of God, which surpasses all understanding, will guard your hearts and your minds in Christ Jesus."

My reflections on being a Grandparent

The fifth month of pregnancy

_____

_____

_____

_____

_____

_____

Giving thanks to God for having created my grandbaby

A prayer in my own words

_____

_____

_____

_____

_____

_____

_____

_____

_____

_____

A Nine-Month Novena

To pray each day throughout this month

Dear Lord Jesus, Blessed Mother Mary, and all of the angels and saints, please hear my prayer. First, I desire to express my deep gratitude for the blessing of being chosen as a grandmother. I earnestly ask that while I pray for my precious unborn grandchild during this nine-month journey of growth in the womb, that you would watch over me and teach me. I desire to come ever closer to God so that I may become a dazzling example of Christian love to my grandchild—lighting the path to heaven. I pray that the love of God will continually radiate from my heart to touch the hearts of others, especially to all in my family. Thank you, dear Lord, for your abiding love! Amen.

Faithfully Praying

Yet she will be saved through childbearing,
provided they continue in faith and love and holiness, with modesty.
—1 TIMOTHY 2:15

Faith is a powerful word. But it can be mysterious too. We often hear about folks who took a "leap of faith" in one endeavor or another. But living by faith is not an easy thing. One time the apostles begged Jesus, "Increase our faith!" Jesus told them straight out, "If you had faith the size of a mustard seed, you could say to this mulberry tree, 'Be uprooted and planted in the sea,' and it would obey you" (Luke 17:5–6).

Wow. Do we have that kind of faith? Perhaps for most of us, our faith is not even the size of a mustard seed—and that is pretty tiny! However, there is something we can do about it. Allow me to share a precious story.

I remember well my little second-grader when she was in faith formation class. I was teaching about the Eucharist, and young Felicia couldn't contain any longer the sentiments that had been burning in her heart. She felt ready to burst. So, she shot out from behind her desk and rushed to the front of the class. She motioned for me to bend my head down and she whispered something pretty incredible in my ear. It was just two simple, yet profound statements.

"I believe. But I want to believe MORE!"

That was it. Yet, her pure and earnest desire for an increase in faith touched my heart. I told her that I would talk to her about it after class since she didn't want her peers to know what she had expressed to me. We had a nice talk afterwards, and I believe that Felicia's worries were addressed and she felt consoled. Felicia's innocent and pure desire expressed to me that day has forever stuck with me.

"I believe. But I want to believe more." Do we feel that way? Do we want more faith?

Jesus told St. Paul, "My grace is sufficient for you, for power is made perfect in weakness." And Paul tells us, "So, I will boast all the more gladly of my weaknesses, so that the power of Christ may dwell in me . . . for whenever I am weak, then I am strong" (2 Corinthians 12:9–10).

Let's be like Felicia in her childlike desire and pray for that increase in faith. Don't be so hard on yourself for the times you haven't had much faith. But trust Our Lord that he will provide sufficient graces when you ask. Whenever we are weak, we can be strong in the Lord.

Throughout this sixth month with your grandchild in the womb, do your best to pray many faithful prayers. As you are doing so, ask God to increase that beautiful virtue of faith that was gifted to you at your baptism. And let's take a look at your grandbaby's progress thus far.

Discovering My Grandbaby's Developments

Your unborn grandbaby is nearly fully formed. The head is almost proportional to the body, and the face is fully developed. However, your grandchild's eyes are still fused shut, but he or she can sense light and dark. Soon, the blinking will begin! The organs are still developing and the lungs are not fully developed. Your grandbaby measures about 9 inches to a foot long from the top of the head to the rump and weighs about 2 pounds. He or she can hiccup (mom might feel this) and cough. Baby is producing white blood cells to help fight off diseases.

His or her skin is no longer translucent, and fat is building up under the skin. Muscles are getting stronger, and mom might be able to tell this by the baby's kicks and wiggles. Your unborn grandbaby might respond to loud sounds or voices by moving in response. This month your little one develops unique fingerprints and toe prints!

My hope and prayer for my grandchild this month
In my own words

_____

_____

_____

_____

_____

_____

_____

Holy Insights

GOOD SAINT JOSEPH!

Let's talk about St. Joseph, who seems to have been extremely quiet according to the lack of his words recorded in Scripture. For someone so quiet, how did he come to be known as the Universal Patron for the Church? St. Joseph may have seemed extraordinarily silent and unassuming, but we know that God relied on him to take care of Mary and Jesus with a steadfast faith—totally attentive to the promptings of the Holy Spirit. God knew that Joseph was the man for the job.

Let's step back about 2,000 years ago to a city of Galilee named Nazareth when Joseph, a just man, did not want his betrothed, Mary, to be put to shame and therefore decided to leave her quietly after finding out about her pregnancy.

An angel appeared to Joseph in a dream and said to him, "Joseph, son of David, do not be afraid to take Mary as your wife, for the child conceived in her is from the Holy Spirit. She will bear a son, and you are to name him Jesus, for he will save his people from their sins." We can't even begin to imagine what went through Joseph's mind in that moment, or what initially transpired in his heart and soul.

However, we do know what Joseph immediately chose to do. Scripture tells us that when Joseph woke up from that pivotal dream, he did exactly as the angel instructed. He took Mary as his wife (Matthew 1:24). St. Joseph acted on faith and united himself with the faith of Mary. No doubt that virtue continued to grow in his heart and soul.

Before the angel Gabriel visited Joseph, did Joseph suspect wrongdoing on Mary's part? Was Joseph confused? Or, could Joseph have been completely awestruck by the work of the Holy Spirit in Mary and felt unworthy to remain with her? Through the ages, there have been many interpretations expressed about why Joseph would wish to separate himself from Mary.

St. John Paul II gives his voice to this in *Guardian of the Redeemer*: "Even though he decided to draw back so as not to interfere in the plan of God which was coming to pass in Mary, Joseph obeyed the explicit command of the angel and took Mary into his home, while respecting the fact that she belonged exclusively to God."[17] The pontiff's deduction seems crystal clear. As a just man, Joseph was simply trying to do the will of God, and as much as he loved Mary, he would get out of the way if that was necessary.

Servant of God Fr. John A. Hardon, SJ, said, "Saint Joseph was a very humble man. He recognized his place with respect to Mary and Jesus. He knew that he was inferior to both of them in the order of grace. Yet he accepted his role as spouse of Mary and guardian of the Son of God."[18]

In his Apostolic Exhortation *Redemptoris Custos*, St. John Paul II points out that it is evident that God chose Joseph to be the foster-father of Jesus when the angel appeared to him: "It is to Joseph, then, that the messenger turns, entrusting to him the responsibilities of an earthly father with regard to Mary's Son." He further explained that the humble saint showed a readiness of will. "He took her in all the mystery of her motherhood. He took her together with the Son who had come into the world by the power of the Holy Spirit. In this way he showed a readiness of will like Mary's with regard to what God asked of him through the angel."

We can ponder St. John Paul II's words in which he tells us how the silence of Joseph actually reveals his contemplative soul. Specifically: "The same aura of silence that envelops everything else about Joseph also shrouds his work as a carpenter in the house of Nazareth." But, it's much more than that. He explained, "It is, however, a silence that reveals in a special way the inner portrait of the man. The Gospels speak exclusively of what Joseph 'did.' Still, they allow us to discover in his 'actions' - shrouded in silence as they are - an aura of deep contemplation. Joseph was in daily contact with the mystery 'hidden from ages past,' and which 'dwelt' under his roof." St. John Paul II added, "This explains, for example, why

St. Teresa of Jesus, the great reformer of the Carmelites, promoted the renewal of veneration to St. Joseph in Western Christianity."[19]

We should turn to St. Joseph in all of our needs. I turn to him regularly and encourage others to do so since he is quick to answer our prayers and help us with the needs in the family.

Now, offer to God your heartfelt prayers.

Swaddling with Saint Anne Prayer

Dear St. Anne, mother of the Mother of Jesus, I pray that I may unite my heartfelt prayer to yours and that you will present it before the throne of God. For so long you and Joachim prayed for a child. God granted your request in a miraculous way, since you were infertile. As well, God gifted you with the great Mother of God! Surely, you prayed earnestly for your daughter, Mary, during your pregnancy with her in your womb. You must have also prayed during the pregnancy of the Lord Jesus, when he resided in your daughter's womb—his first tabernacle. Please assist me along my own prayer journey awaiting the birth of my grandchild. Pray that I can become more holy throughout this nine-month novena. Please help me to swaddle my unborn grandbaby in loving prayer, together with you, so that he or she will be safe and well, according to God's holy will. Amen.

Mama Mary Cradling Prayer

Dear Mother Mary, Mother of Jesus and my Mother, please help me to unite my prayers with yours. My heart is stirred with love, contemplating that our Lord Jesus resided in your holy womb for nine months. You experienced his growth and blessed movements. I can imagine St. Joseph gently placing his weathered hand lovingly on your abdomen to feel your Son's motions and life. Please ask your Son, Jesus, to watch over my unborn grandchild, his or her mother, and me. Please help me to cradle my unborn grandbaby in loving prayer with you and St. Joseph so that my grandchild will be safe and well, according to God's holy will. *Hail Mary*, Amen.

Just What the Doctor Ordered

To be a Catholic grandmother means to be part of the great Communion of Saints! Earlier, we discussed how the gift of faith affects our lives. As well, we learned a bit about good St. Joseph, who lived and breathed his faith. Throughout this month, take time to prayerfully connect with the saints, especially St. Joseph, along this marvelous journey as your unborn grandbaby is growing within its mother's womb!

Preparing with the Saints

GOOD SAINT JOSEPH

What made St. Joseph tick? We can learn much about his attributes or qualities by reading or praying the Litany of St. Joseph, which lists twenty-five invocations. We could learn about his humility, chastity, and obedience; his prudence; and his great love for Our Lord and Mary and Jesus. Let's take a look at his love.

Servant of God Fr. John A. Hardon, SJ, said we should greatly admire all of the wonderful virtues of St. Joseph, "but he is to be especially imitated in his love for Jesus and Mary." Fr. Hardon explained why. He said, St. Joseph "was placed into their lives by an all-wise Providence and lived up to God's expectations by giving them his deepest attention and care."

That doesn't happen naturally. We need to move our will to be good to someone, even our family members. Now, of course we are talking about the Holy Family, not just any family. Still, Fr. Hardon points out that Joseph put his love into action. Specifically, he explains, "What most bears emphasis is not so much that Jesus and Mary were physically so close to Saint Joseph. He was in their company day after day for many years. It was rather that Joseph put his love into practice. Joseph put his love to work. He did not merely tell Jesus and Mary that he loved them. He acted out his love." Fr. Hardon drove his point further—"He lived it. That is the secret of true love. We are as truly devoted to Christ and His Mother as we do what we know they want us to do."

What might that be? Fr. Hardon suggests that "It is to see God's providence in everything that enters our lives." He gives examples. We can ponder his suggestions:

- In disappointments and failures.
- In unexpected turns of events.
- In frustrating delays.
- In unwanted demands on our time.
- In the strange behavior of some people.
- In "the mysterious silence of God who often hides the purpose he has and yet tells us, through people—that is the key, through people—what he wants us to do."[20]

Get to know St. Joseph and ask for his help.

St. John Paul II said St. Joseph is a great role model for fathers, especially in a time of a "fatherless society." He said, "We notice ever more clearly the need to be able to count on fathers who can fulfill their role, combining tenderness with seriousness, understanding with strictness, camaraderie with the exercise of authority, because only in this way will children be able to grow harmoniously, overcoming their fears and preparing themselves to meet courageously the unknown factors in life."

The late pontiff encouraged modern families to look to the Holy Family for help and to rediscover joy within the family:

And you, families of today, who are experiencing rapid changes in modern society and suffering their sometimes worrying repercussions, you can find in the family of Nazareth, which Joseph watched over with anxious care, the ever-present model of a community of persons in which love assures an understanding that is daily renewed. Invoking

Jesus, Mary and Joseph, the members of every family of your ecclesial communities can rediscover in the various moments of their lives the joy of the reciprocal gift, the comfort of solidarity in trials, the serene peace of those who know how to count on the omnipotent, even if mysterious, Divine Providence.[21]

St. Teresa of Avila, who also often extolled the power of St. Joseph, stated: "Our Lord would have us understand that as He was subject to St. Joseph on earth—for Joseph, bearing the title of father and being His guardian, could command Him—so now in Heaven Our Lord grants all his petitions. I have asked others to recommend themselves to St. Joseph, and they too, know the same thing by experience. . . ."[22] You can heed St. Teresa's advice by recommending yourself and your unborn grandchild to St. Joseph's care.

Saint Joseph Pregnancy Prayer

Dear St. Joseph, though you remained quiet, you were very heroic and full of God's grace. You were ever attentive to the Holy Spirit and acted upon faith while courageously and lovingly caring for the Holy Family. The saints praise you as a powerful intercessor! St. Teresa of Avila said you never failed to help her. Please look kindly upon my cherished unborn grandchild and beseech our dear Lord to protect his or her precious life, as well as the life of his or her mother. Please help me to grow in holiness throughout this nine-month novena for my grandchild. Amen.

As well, let us ask St. Joseph in the words of Pope Leo XIII:

Most beloved father, dispel the evil of falsehood and sin . . . graciously assist us from heaven in our struggle with the powers of darkness . . . and just as once you saved the Child Jesus from mortal danger, so now defend God's holy Church from the snares of her enemies and from all adversity. Amen.

Memorare to Saint Joseph[23]

Remember, most pure spouse of Mary, ever Virgin, my loving protector, St. Joseph, that no one ever had recourse to your protection or asked for your aid without obtaining relief. Confiding, therefore, in your goodness, I come before you and humbly implore you. Despise not my petitions, foster-father of the Redeemer, but graciously receive them. Amen.

Memorare to Mary

Remember, O most gracious Virgin Mary, that never was it known that anyone who fled to thy protection, implored thy help, or sought thine intercession was left unaided. Inspired by this confidence, I fly unto thee, O Virgin of virgins, my mother; to thee do I come, before thee I stand, sinful and sorrowful. O Mother of the Word Incarnate, despise not my petitions, but in thy mercy hear and answer me. Amen.

Prayer to the Holy Family

Lord Jesus Christ, being subject to Mary and Joseph, you sanctified family life by your beautiful virtues. Grant that we, with the help of Mary and Joseph, may be taught by the example of your holy Family, and may after death enjoy its everlasting companionship. Lord Jesus, help us ever to follow the example of your Holy Family, that in the hour of our death your glorious Virgin Mother together with St. Joseph may come to meet us, and we may be worthy to be received by you into the everlasting joys of heaven. You live and reign forever. Amen.

To Ponder in Your Heart

Take some time this sixth month of your grandchild's development to ponder the following words from Scripture: "So we do not lose heart. Even though our outer nature is wasting away, our inner nature is being renewed day by day. For this slight momentary affliction is preparing us for an eternal weight of glory beyond all measure, because we look not at what can be seen but at what cannot be seen; for what can be seen is temporary, but what cannot be seen is eternal" (2 Corinthians 4:16–18). Strive to look beyond what is "momentary" and what "can be seen." Prepare your heart for everlasting life. Now is the time!

My reflections on being a Grandparent
The sixth month of pregnancy

Giving thanks to God for having created my grandbaby

A prayer in my own words

Nine-Month Novena

To pray each day throughout this month

Dear Lord Jesus, Blessed Mother Mary, and all of the angels and saints, please hear my prayer. First, I desire to express my deep gratitude for the blessing of being chosen as a grandmother. I earnestly ask that while I pray for my precious unborn grandchild during this nine-month journey of growth in the womb, that you would watch over me and teach me. I desire to come ever closer to God so that I may become a dazzling example of Christian love to my grandchild—lighting the path to heaven. I pray that the love of God will continually radiate from my heart to touch the hearts of others, especially to all in my family. Thank you, dear Lord, for your abiding love! Amen.

Steadfast in Prayer

Devote yourselves to prayer, keeping alert in it with thanksgiving.
—COLOSSIANS 4:2

I know that you want to be steadfast in praying for your unborn grandchild. And, don't forget—with *thanksgiving*. Whether you are close by and can visit and check on mom (with the protruding abdomen), or are praying from afar, your loving and steadfast prayers will greatly benefit her and your grandbaby.

It is wise to form solid habits of prayer. If we don't form prayer habits, we might not pray at all. Or, at best, we might resort to prayer as a last-ditch effort for something—*using* God, rather than loving and trusting him. Hopefully, by praying through this book you have formed the habit of praying throughout your unborn child's growth in the womb. You will also hopefully have developed a good habit of pausing here and there to meditate along this journey—this nine-month novena of prayer in which you are writing down your own prayers and reflections about your grandchild as he or she continues to grow and get ready for birth.

God willing, your prayer habits will be passed down to your grandchild!

Throughout this seventh month in the womb, strive to pray many steadfast prayers of gratitude for your unborn grandchild. And let's take a look at your grandbaby's progress.

Discovering My Grandbaby's Developments

By the end of this month in the womb your grandchild will be almost three pounds and will be about a foot long. He or she can now open and close his or her eyes! The organs are rapidly growing and maturing, getting ready for life outside the womb. The lungs are developing and beginning to produce a substance called surfactant which will allow the proper expansion of the lungs. Under your grand-baby's skin extra fat is developing, to fill out all of the wrinkles and supply energy and insulation. Skin cells are producing the pigments that give skin color. Your grandchild is getting closer to when he or she will make a grand entrance into the world!

My hope and prayer for my grandchild this month

In my own words

_____

_____

_____

_____

_____

_____

_____

_____

_____

_____

_____

_____

_____

Holy Insights

There are so many reasons we give for not praying as much as we should. People busy themselves with so many things and then chalk it up to thinking that they just don't have the time to pray. I might be preaching to the choir here: grandmothers tend to be champions of prayer! Yet, because I know that you have influence over others, especially your family, I think it's an important subject for us to ponder as Christians who can help others find a healthy balance in their lives—adults and children alike.

We might consider the beautiful encounters with God that were lost when one has taken far too long on the internet or some form of technology. Consider the lovely and meaningful litanies that could have been prayed had you not run out of time. The list could go on. Let's not make excuses or lose our attention. Prayer is a gift from God.

The Catechism teaches that we must be humble to pray:

> "Prayer is the raising of one's mind and heart to God or the requesting of good things from God." But when we pray, do we speak from the height of our pride and will, or "out of the depths" of a humble and contrite heart? He who humbles himself will be exalted; *humility* is the foundation of prayer. Only when we humbly acknowledge that "we do not know how to pray as we ought," are we ready to receive freely the gift of prayer. "Man is a beggar before God." (CCC #2559)

As well, we can pray in words or gestures.

> Whether prayer is expressed in words or gestures, it is the whole man who prays. But in naming the source of prayer, Scripture speaks sometimes of the soul or the spirit, but most often of the heart (more than a thousand times). According to Scripture, it is the *heart* that prays. If our heart is far from God, the words of prayer are in vain. (CCC #2562)

We should ponder whether or not our prayers rise from our heart. Is our heart contrite and sincere? Or is it far from God? Do we know someone far from God? How might our heartfelt prayers help them? The Catechism speaks about our heart as a place to which to withdraw and from which we pray:

> The heart is the dwelling-place where I am, where I live; according to the Semitic or Biblical expression, the heart is the place "to which I withdraw." The heart is our hidden center, beyond the grasp of our reason and of others; only the Spirit of God can fathom the human heart and know it fully. The heart is the place of decision, deeper than our psychic drives. It is the place of truth, where we choose life or death. It is the place of encounter, because as image of God we live in relation: it is the place of covenant. (CCC #2563)

I encourage you to spend more time in prayer, offering your heart up often throughout the day. Try to form those good prayer habits and teach them to the children. Now, offer to God your heartfelt prayer for your unborn grandchild.

Swaddling with Saint Anne Prayer

Dear St. Anne, mother of the Mother of Jesus, I pray that I may unite my heartfelt prayer to yours and that you will present it before the throne of God. For so long you and Joachim prayed for a child. God granted your request in a miraculous way, since you were infertile. As well, God gifted you with the great Mother of God! Surely, you prayed earnestly for your daughter, Mary, during your pregnancy with her in your womb. You must have also prayed during the pregnancy of the Lord Jesus, when he resided in your daughter's womb—his first tabernacle. Please assist me along my own prayer journey awaiting the birth of my grandchild. Pray that I can become more holy throughout this nine-month novena. Please help me to swaddle my unborn grandbaby in loving prayer, together with you, so that he or she will be safe and well, according to God's holy will. Amen.

Mama Mary Cradling Prayer

Dear Mother Mary, Mother of Jesus and my Mother, please help me to unite my prayers with yours. My heart is stirred with love, contemplating that our Lord Jesus resided in your holy womb for nine months. You experienced his growth and blessed movements. I can imagine St. Joseph gently placing his weathered hand lovingly on your abdomen to feel your Son's motions and life. Please ask your Son, Jesus, to watch over my unborn grandchild, his or her mother, and me. Please help me to cradle my unborn grandbaby in loving prayer with you and St. Joseph so that my grandchild will be safe and well, according to God's holy will. *Hail Mary*, Amen.

Just What the Doctor Ordered

We will never fully realize the blessings of prayer until we get to heaven. All of those countless prayers for our family members surely must be a delight to the heart of God! Relish in your joyful and earnest prayer times throughout this month, prayerfully awaiting your sweet grandbaby.

Preparing with the Saints

THE SAINTS AND PRAYER

We can learn so much about prayer from the saints. I love how St. Thérèse of Lisieux described prayer: "For me, prayer is a surge of the heart; it is a simple look turned toward heaven, it is a cry of recognition and of love, embracing both trial and joy." She was a simple soul, yet she has been declared a Doctor of the Church! Her example of humility and simplicity can indeed help us in our own prayer lives.

St. Augustine told us, "Prayer is the encounter of God's thirsts with ours." His statement is succinct yet powerful. Do we thirst for God? Do we fully realize that

God actually thirsts for our love? It might take a lifetime and then some to fully comprehend that Almighty God thirsts for us—for me—individually, apart from anyone else. And, he is God! Yet, he is constantly seeking to encounter us and searches us out when we turn our backs on him or try to hide from him. Like the Samaritan woman who accidentally met Jesus at the well when she showed up there at noon, the hottest part of the day, possibly trying to avoid everyone. This famous encounter is the one to which St. Augustine refers.

In speaking about the Samaritan woman at the well and Our Lord's thirst for us, Pope Emeritus Benedict XVI said: "The omnipotence of Love always respects human freedom; it knocks at the door of man's heart and waits patiently for his answer." He went on, encouraging the faithful: "Each one of us can identify himself with the Samaritan woman: Jesus is waiting for us . . . to speak to our hearts, to my heart. Let us pause. . . . Let us listen to his voice which tells us, 'If you knew the gift of God.' May the Virgin help us not to miss this appointment, on which our true happiness depends."[24]

God does not force himself upon us, but he always thirsts for us.

St. Teresa of Calcutta meditated long and hard on the words "I thirst." The thirst of Jesus from the cross was so important to the petite saint of the gutters that she made sure those two words were painted on the wall of every one of her convent's chapels all around the world. I have seen them in a half dozen of those chapels.

Mother Teresa once gave to me a little card with these words: "The fruit of silence is prayer, the fruit of prayer is faith, the fruit of faith is love, the fruit of love is service, and the fruit of service is peace." I have kept that card in my prayer book. It is very worn but it remains a wonderful reminder to me to carve out time for silence in my life. There, in some kind of quiet, I should immerse my heart and pray. If I strive to do this on a regular basis, the fruits that Mother Teresa wrote about will blossom in my heart to be shared with others.

St. Faustina wrote in her *Diary,* "There is no soul which is not bound to pray, for every single grace comes to the soul through prayer."[25] Let us be sure to search out periods of silence into which we can retreat in our hearts to enjoy beautiful conversations with our Lord. He awaits our encounters. He thirsts for our love.

Saint Joseph Pregnancy Prayer

Dear St. Joseph, though you remained quiet, you were very heroic and full of God's grace. You were ever attentive to the Holy Spirit and acted upon faith while courageously and lovingly caring for the Holy Family. The saints praise you as a powerful intercessor! St. Teresa of Avila said you never failed to help her. Please look kindly upon my cherished unborn grandchild and beseech our dear Lord to protect his or her precious life, as well as the life of his or her mother. Please help me to grow in holiness throughout this nine-month novena for my grandchild. Amen.

Memorare to Saint Joseph[26]

Remember, most pure spouse of Mary, ever Virgin, my loving protector, St. Joseph, that no one ever had recourse to your protection or asked for your aid without obtaining relief. Confiding, therefore, in your goodness, I come before you and humbly implore you. Despise not my petitions, foster-father of the Redeemer, but graciously receive them. Amen.

Memorare to Mary

Remember, O most gracious Virgin Mary, that never was it known that anyone who fled to thy protection, implored thy help, or sought thine intercession was left unaided. Inspired by this confidence, I fly unto thee, O Virgin of virgins, my mother; to thee do I come, before thee I stand, sinful and sorrowful. O Mother of the Word Incarnate, despise not my petitions, but in thy mercy hear and answer me. Amen.

Prayer to the Holy Family

Lord Jesus Christ, being subject to Mary and Joseph, you sanctified family life by your beautiful virtues. Grant that we, with the help of Mary and Joseph, may be taught by the example of your holy Family, and may after death enjoy its everlasting companionship. Lord Jesus, help us ever to follow the example of your Holy Family, that in the hour of our death your glorious Virgin Mother together with St. Joseph may come to meet us, and we may be worthy to be received by you into the everlasting joys of heaven. You live and reign forever. Amen.

To Ponder in Your Heart

During this seventh month of your grandchild's time in utero, pause to ponder these words: "It is the *heart* that prays. If our heart is far from God, the words of prayer are in vain" (CCC #2562). Ask yourself, *Is my heart praying? Do I thirst for God?* Several times this month, take five or ten minutes to pause, close your eyes, and ponder this. Ask God to tell you, to help you.

My reflections on being a Grandparent

The seventh month of pregnancy

_____

_____

_____

_____

_____

_____

Giving thanks to God for having created my grandbaby

A prayer in my own words

Nine-Month Novena

To pray each day throughout this month

Dear Lord Jesus, Blessed Mother Mary, and all of the angels and saints, please hear my prayer. First, I desire to express my deep gratitude for the blessing of being chosen as a grandmother. I earnestly ask that while I pray for my precious unborn grandchild during this nine-month journey of growth in the womb, that you would watch over me and teach me. I desire to come ever closer to God so that I may become a dazzling example of Christian love to my grandchild—lighting the path to heaven. I pray that the love of God will continually radiate from my heart to touch the hearts of others, especially to all in my family. Thank you, dear Lord, for your abiding love! Amen.

EIGHTH MONTH IN UTERO

Earnestly Praying

Do not fear, for I am with you, do not be afraid,
for I am your God;
I will strengthen you, I will help you,
I will uphold you with my victorious right hand.
—ISAIAH 41:10

Your unborn grandchild has been growing in leaps and bounds. I'm sure that mom has been feeling those leaps and bounds! I remember well my babies in utero, and at times I wondered if they would become gymnasts or acrobats! Their movements within me warmed my heart, knowing that my baby was there, but also at times the sudden movements or kicks up high in my rib cage caused me to jump!

Our verse above speaks about not being afraid. God tells us he will strengthen us and help us. I wonder how many times even in the course of a day we become fearful or worried about something. It's only natural as a parent and grandparent that we are concerned about our families. But I believe that worry is different from being concerned. When we worry, we might become obsessed with a lack of control over the problem. Some say that worry is a sin. While worry in itself might not necessarily be sinful, by worrying, we in essence are telling God that we don't trust him with our lives.

The Bible tells us, "Do not worry about anything, but in everything by prayer and supplication with thanksgiving let your requests be made known to God. And the peace of God, which surpasses all understanding, will guard your hearts and your minds in Christ Jesus" (Philippians 4:6–7). We need God's peace. We can strive to continuously hand our worry and fears over to God. At times this will be more challenging than at other times.

As well, we read in 1 Peter 5:6–8, "Humble yourselves therefore under the mighty hand of God, so that he may exalt you in due time. Cast all your anxiety on him, because he cares for you. Discipline yourselves, keep alert. Like a roaring lion your adversary the devil prowls around, looking for someone to devour." It would seem that casting our anxiety on God will help us become more able to protect ourselves and our families from the roaring lion. What do you think?

We all struggle with some sort of anxiety or another, but we should give all of our anxiety to God—hand it to him in prayer. When worry comes visiting we can allow it to trigger a response in us to pray and to surrender our worries to God. Getting into the habit of turning to prayer as soon as we can when we are deeply concerned or worried will be a great benefit to our minds, hearts, and souls, and to all whom we care for.

Finally, we are heartily encouraged, "Look at the birds of the air; they neither sow nor reap nor gather into barns, and yet your heavenly Father feeds them. Are you not of more value than they? And can any of you by worrying add a single hour to your span of life? And why do you worry about clothing? Consider the lilies of the field, how they grow; they neither toil nor spin, yet I tell you, even Solomon in all his glory was not clothed like one of these" (Matthew 6: 26–29). We need to trust God that if he cares so much for all of his other creations, how much more does he care for us whom he gifted with an eternal soul. God wants us to trust him wholeheartedly.

Throughout this eighth month of your grandchild's growth in the womb, strive to pray earnest prayers of gratitude as you turn any anxiety over to God. And let's take a look at your grandbaby's progress.

Discovering My Grandbaby's Developments

A lot happens during the eighth month. That baby is quickly putting on weight and gaining body fat reserves. He or she might be more active and kicking. Mom begins to feel distinct movements and even hiccups! He or she is probably about

18 inches long and five or so pounds. The fine body hair called lanugo that has covered his or her petite body is now beginning to disappear as hair on the head is starting to grow. This month brings much brain development, and your little grandchild can see and hear. Baby's bones have begun to harden, with the exception of the head, which needs to pass through the birth canal safely.

My hope and prayer for my grandchild this month
In my own words

"BE NOT AFRAID"

To be afraid or not to be afraid reminds me so much of St. John Paul II, the incredible pope whose memory is still vivid in many of our hearts. We recall that as soon as he became pope, he encouraged the faithful to "Be not afraid" and would continue to do so all throughout his pontificate. He spoke these words for the first time on October 22, 1978, in St. Peter's Square:

> Brothers and sisters, do not be afraid to welcome Christ and accept his power. Help the Pope and all those who wish to serve Christ and with Christ's power to serve the human person and the whole of mankind. Be not afraid. Open wide the doors for Christ. To his saving power open the boundaries of States, economic and political systems, the vast fields of culture, civilization and development. Be not afraid. Christ knows "what is in man." He alone knows it.[27]

Later on, in his book *Crossing the Threshold of Hope,* the pontiff spoke about those holy words of encouragement that he uttered at the very beginning of his pontificate, and he gave us reason to feel consoled:

> When, on October 22, 1978, I said the words "Be not afraid!" in St. Peter's Square, I could not fully know how far they would take me and the entire Church. Their meaning came more from the Holy Spirit, the Consoler, promised by the Lord Jesus to His disciples, than from the man who spoke them. Nevertheless, with the passing of the years, I have recalled these words on many occasions. . . . Why should we have no fear? Because man has been redeemed by God. . . . *The power of Christ's Cross and Resurrection is greater than any evil which man could or should fear.*[28]

St. John Paul II was a soul who trusted the Lord. On June 7, 1997, he visited the Shrine of Divine Mercy in Krakow, Poland, and spoke about the Image of Divine Mercy and trusting in Jesus:

And it is a *message that is clear and understandable for everyone.* Anyone can come here, look at this image of the merciful Jesus, His Heart radiating grace, and hear in the depths of his own soul what Blessed Faustina heard: "*Fear nothing. I am with you always.*"[29]

And if this person responds with a sincere heart: "*Jesus, I trust in You,*" he will find comfort in all his anxieties and fears. In this "dialogue of abandonment," there is established between man and Christ a *special bond that sets love free.* And "there is no fear in love, but perfect love casts out fear" (1 Jn. 4:18).[30]

Heed St. John Paul II's wise words this month to trust Jesus with a sincere heart, allowing him to give you comfort in all of your anxieties and fears. Now, offer to God your heartfelt prayers.

Swaddling with Saint Anne Prayer

Dear St. Anne, mother of the Mother of Jesus, I pray that I may unite my heartfelt prayer to yours and that you will present it before the throne of God. For so long you and Joachim prayed for a child. God granted your request in a miraculous way, since you were infertile. As well, God gifted you with the great Mother of God! Surely, you prayed earnestly for your daughter, Mary, during your pregnancy with her in your womb. You must have also prayed during the pregnancy of the Lord Jesus, when he resided in your daughter's womb–his first tabernacle. Please assist me along my own prayer journey awaiting the birth of my grandchild. Pray that I can become more holy throughout this nine-month novena. Please help me to swaddle my unborn grandbaby in loving prayer, together with you, so that he or she will be safe and well, according to God's holy will. Amen.

Mama Mary Cradling Prayer

Dear Mother Mary, Mother of Jesus and my Mother, please help me to unite my prayers with yours. My heart is stirred with love, contemplating that our Lord Jesus resided in your holy womb for nine months. You experienced his growth and blessed movements. I can imagine St. Joseph gently placing his weathered hand lovingly on your abdomen to feel your Son's motions and life. Please ask your Son, Jesus, to watch over my unborn grandchild, his or her mother, and me. Please help me to cradle my unborn grandbaby in loving prayer with you and St. Joseph so that my grandchild will be safe and well, according to God's holy will. *Hail Mary,* Amen.

Just What the Doctor Ordered

It won't be too much longer now before your precious grandbaby is born. Try your best to hand all of your worries and concerns over to God. Keep praying and, most of all, trust God.

Jesus, I trust in YOU!

Preparing with the Saints

SAINT FAUSTINA AND TRUSTING GOD

It was to St. Faustina that Jesus entrusted the mission of Divine Mercy. The mercy of Jesus was not a new revelation. However, in February 1931, in Plock, Poland, Jesus appeared to St. Faustina, a novice in the Congregation of the Sisters of Mercy, to reveal his mercy in a new way. He desired that people would trust in his great mercy and love and would also show mercy to others.

Jesus appeared to St. Faustina in her cell. He was clothed in white and had one hand raised in blessing while the other was touching his garment at the breast. Two large rays emanated from beneath the garment. One was red and the other was pale. St. Faustina was struck with joyful awe, took it all in, and recorded the details in her *Diary*. Jesus explained the mission to her:

Paint an image according to the pattern you see, with the signature: Jesus, I trust in You. I promise that the soul that will venerate this image will not perish. I also promise victory over [its] enemies already here on earth, especially at the hour of death. I Myself will defend it as My own glory.[31]

Jesus would later reveal to St. Faustina the many extraordinary graces that would come through the image, and He would drive home the importance of showing mercy to others:

By means of this image I shall grant many graces to souls. It is to be a reminder of the demands of My mercy, because even the strongest faith is of no avail without works.[32]

Now, just because Jesus entrusted the message of Divine Mercy to the young novice does not mean that the journey in carrying it out was to be blissful or effortless. Far from it! More than a simple *entrustment*, it was a holy *burden* placed in her heart and upon her shoulders. As is often the case with visionaries, no one believes them! Even their superiors. Their heart is bursting with a precious supernatural gift that they passionately desire to get out to the world according to heaven's instructions, but, alas, it seems impossible. The process is laborious and even painful at times. However, through patience and prayer, St. Faustina learned to wholeheartedly trust God with every detail. As the signature of the Divine Mercy image states: "Jesus, I trust in You."

On our own, without God, we cannot accomplish anything. With God, all things are possible. St. Faustina knew that. Certainly, we are not all called to carry out such great missions. Yet, each of us in all of our walks of life is entrusted with some sort of a mission. Most importantly, it is in the bright light of faith that we will radiate for our families through our loving prayers, teachings, and example. Along the way, let's be mindful of what Jesus told St. Faustina and the world. The Divine Mercy Image "is to be a reminder of the demands of My mercy, because even the strongest faith is of no avail without works."

Saint Joseph Pregnancy Prayer

Dear St. Joseph, though you remained quiet, you were very heroic and full of God's grace. You were ever attentive to the Holy Spirit and acted upon faith while courageously and lovingly caring for the Holy Family. The saints praise you as a powerful intercessor! St. Teresa of Avila said you never failed to help her. Please look kindly upon my cherished unborn grandchild and beseech our dear Lord to protect his or her precious life, as well as the life of his or her mother. Please help me to grow in holiness throughout this nine-month novena for my grandchild. Amen.

Memorare to Saint Joseph[33]

Remember, most pure spouse of Mary, ever Virgin, my loving protector, St. Joseph, that no one ever had recourse to your protection or asked for your aid without obtaining relief. Confiding, therefore, in your goodness, I come before you and humbly implore you. Despise not my petitions, foster-father of the Redeemer, but graciously receive them. Amen.

Memorare to Mary

Remember, O most gracious Virgin Mary, that never was it known that anyone who fled to thy protection, implored thy help, or sought thine intercession was left unaided. Inspired by this confidence, I fly unto thee, O Virgin of virgins, my mother; to thee do I come, before thee I stand, sinful and sorrowful. O Mother of the Word Incarnate, despise not my petitions, but in thy mercy hear and answer me. Amen.

Prayer to the Holy Family

Lord Jesus Christ, being subject to Mary and Joseph, you sanctified family life by your beautiful virtues. Grant that we, with the help of Mary and Joseph, may be taught by the example of your holy Family, and may after death enjoy its everlasting companionship. Lord Jesus, help us ever to follow the example of your Holy Family, that in the hour of our death your glorious Virgin Mother together with St. Joseph may come to meet us, and we may be worthy to be received by you into the everlasting joys of heaven. You live and reign forever. Amen.

To Ponder in Your Heart

"Jesus, I trust in You."

Take time this eighth month of your grandchild's development to ponder the words in the signature of the Divine Mercy image that Jesus himself dictated to his "Secretary of Mercy," St. Faustina Maria Kowalska. Say them over and over sincerely in wholehearted prayer. Strive to give all of your worries to Jesus. Trust him with your life and the life of your unborn grandbaby.

My reflections on being a Grandparent

The eighth month of pregnancy

_____

_____

_____

_____

_____

_____

Giving thanks to God for having created my grand baby

A prayer in my own words

_____

_____

_____

_____

_____

_____

_____

_____

Nine-Month Novena

To pray each day throughout this month

Dear Lord Jesus, Blessed Mother Mary, and all of the angels and saints, please hear my prayer. First, I desire to express my deep gratitude for the blessing of being chosen as a grandmother. I earnestly ask that while I pray for my precious unborn grandchild during this nine-month journey of growth in the womb, that you would watch over me and teach me. I desire to come ever closer to God so that I may become a dazzling example of Christian love to my grandchild–lighting the path to heaven. I pray that the love of God will continually radiate from my heart to touch the hearts of others, especially to all in my family. Thank you, dear Lord, for your abiding love! Amen.

Patiently Waiting!

When a woman is in labor, she has pain, because her hour has come.
But when her child is born, she no longer remembers the anguish
because of the joy of having brought a human being into the world.

—JOHN 16:21

Your unborn grandbaby's development might have seemed to fly by so far. One month leads into another and there are always new changes along the way to keep your attention. However, I am sorry to say, this last month might seem to take f-o-r-e-v-e-r. I know it always did for me as a mom. It has for me as a grandma, too. I could barely wait each time!

When I was an expectant mom, I couldn't wait for that ninth month to be over so I could finally hold my precious newborn against my heart, and so that I could finally feel more comfortable! As a grandma, I simply could not wait to meet my grandchild—a little someone that I had been praying for, but had yet to meet face-to-face, heart-to-heart. Just you wait! There is nothing like it!

Perhaps you'll find enough to do to keep busy this last long month. Maybe you'll even knit, crochet, or sew something for your grandchild, or perhaps craft a patchwork blanket. If you're not crafty, you might be busy looking at baby clothes and things online or in stores. When I was a young mother, I bought many baby clothes from thrift shops. The baby clothes were in perfect condition. They had been worn hardly at all since babies grow so fast. I washed them, folded them up, and waited for my baby to come. I busied myself with getting the nursery ready. Perhaps, if you live close by, you will help mom with that. Or, you might even surprise her with a baby shower.

Throughout this ninth month in the womb, strive to pray many prayers of gratitude as you try to wait patiently. Now, let's take a look at your grandbaby's progress.

Discovering My Grandbaby's Developments

This last month is so important, as your unborn grandbaby grows about a half pound to a pound per week. Baby's reflexes have developed, and he or she will be able to respond to touch, sounds, and light. This is the time when baby might turn head down to prepare for delivery. His or her lungs are nearly developed and maturing rapidly to be able to breathe outside the womb. Your grandchild is not so little any longer. He or she is about 7 pounds and about 20 inches long. It's beginning to be a tight fit in baby's first home, and he or she will move around less.

My hope and prayer for my grandchild this month

In my own words

Holy Insights

THE PRESENCE OF JESUS

What is the most significant gift that Jesus gives to us? It is his love and his presence to us in the Eucharist. He does not leave us alone. Jesus promised us that he will be with us until the "end of the age." He fulfills his promise to us through the Eucharist. Jesus said, "I am with you always, to the end of the age" (Matthew 28:20).

Be comforted in knowing this. St. Thomas Aquinas explained, "It is the law of friendship that friends should live together. . . . Christ has not left us without his bodily presence in this our pilgrimage, but he joins us to himself in this sacrament in the reality of his body and blood."[34] And we read in the Gospel, "While they were eating, Jesus took a loaf of bread, and after blessing it he broke it, gave it to the disciples, and said, 'Take, eat; this is my body.' Then he took a cup, and after giving thanks he gave it to them, saying, 'Drink from it, all of you; for this is my blood of the covenant, which is poured out for many for the forgiveness of sins'" (Matthew 26:26–28). The Church teaches:

With this gift of Christ's presence in our midst, the Church is truly blessed. As Jesus told his disciples, referring to his presence among them, "Amen, I say to you, many prophets and righteous people longed to see what you see but did not see it, and to hear what you hear but did not hear it" (Mt. 13:17). In the Eucharist the Church both receives the gift of Jesus Christ and gives grateful thanks to God for such a blessing. This thanksgiving is the only proper response, for through this gift of himself in the celebration of the Eucharist under the appearances of bread and wine Christ gives us the gift of eternal life.[35]

God gives us the gift of the Eucharist because he loves us. At Mass we are spiritually nourished with the bread of heaven. For Catholics, the Eucharist is our holy sustenance. Our Lord Jesus makes himself vulnerable in the host, and he is also hidden in the tabernacle waiting for our visits.

Our Presence

Speaking of "presence" and "visits," I don't think I'll ever forget the time when I had been visiting my grandson Shepherd and it was time for me to leave. My grandson said something to me that completely melted my heart. As I kissed and hugged him goodbye, after I told him that I had to leave for home, I was surprised by one powerful word that pierced my heart.

"Stay!" he blurted out.

It felt almost impossible to leave at that point. So, we chatted a bit more and then parted after a few more squeeze hugs and a big promise to return soon.

Our loving presence to one another in the family is essential in many ways. We grow together in the blessedness of the family—the domestic church. When we can't be together in person, we are connected through phone calls, video conferencing, and letters and cards. Most especially, we are connected with God's love and our prayers for one another.

Consider getting to the Adoration chapel of your church where Jesus is present in the tabernacle. This month, try to spend extra time with Jesus in the Blessed Sacrament, where you can offer your heartfelt prayers.

Now, offer your special prayers for your unborn grandchild.

Swaddling with Saint Anne Prayer

Dear St. Anne, mother of the Mother of Jesus, I pray that I may unite my heartfelt prayer to yours and that you will present it before the throne of God. For so long you and Joachim prayed for a child. God granted your request in a miraculous way, since you were infertile. As well, God gifted you with the great Mother of God! Surely, you prayed earnestly for your daughter, Mary, during your pregnancy with her in your womb. You must have also prayed during the pregnancy of the Lord Jesus, when he resided in your daughter's womb—his first tabernacle. Please assist me along my own prayer journey awaiting the birth of my grandchild. Pray that I can become more holy throughout this nine-month novena. Please help me to swaddle my unborn grandbaby in loving prayer, together with you, so that he or she will be safe and well, according to God's holy will. Amen.

Mama Mary Cradling Prayer

Dear Mother Mary, Mother of Jesus and my Mother, please help me to unite my prayers with yours. My heart is stirred with love, contemplating that our Lord Jesus resided in your holy womb for nine months. You experienced his growth and blessed movements. I can imagine St. Joseph gently placing his weathered hand lovingly on your abdomen to feel your Son's motions and life. Please ask your Son, Jesus, to watch over my unborn grandchild, his or her mother, and me. Please help me to cradle my unborn grandbaby in loving prayer with you and St. Joseph so that my grandchild will be safe and well, according to God's holy will. *Hail Mary*, Amen.

Just What the Doctor Ordered

Your distinctive presence in your unborn grandchild's life is powerful, whether you live near or far away. Your nine-month novena of loving prayer has enveloped your unborn little one. Keep those prayers going continue throughout his or her life. There is nothing like a grandmother's love! Relish in the amazing blessing of being a grandmother, now, and as you await the birth!

Preparing with the Saints

EUCHARISTIC SAINTS

My former spiritual director, now Servant of God Fr. John A. Hardon, SJ, was devoted to Jesus in the Blessed Sacrament. According to Fr. Hardon, "From the dawn of Christian history, faith in the Holy Eucharist as the living Christ has been continuous." He also pointed out, "Every saint of the Catholic Church has been deeply devoted to the Blessed Sacrament. In fact, there is no sanctity without the Eucharist."[36]

Father Hardon explained that the saints "realize that the Holy Eucharist is a sacrament three times over: as Sacrifice Sacrament of the Mass, Communion Sacrament of Holy Communion, and Presence Sacrament."

Let's take a look at a few other saints deeply devoted to and associated with the Eucharist:

- St. Thérèse of Lisieux: Very succinctly, the humble "Little Flower" stated, "The best means to reach perfection is through receiving Holy Communion frequently. Experience sufficiently proves it in those who practice it." She tells us that receiving Jesus in the Eucharist will indeed aid our growth in holiness.

- St. Cyril of Jerusalem: A Doctor of the Church, he was Bishop of Jerusalem in the fourth century. He wrote extensively on the Holy Eucharist. Father Hardon stated about St. Cyril, "His most important writing was the catechetical compendium which has become the standard for all catechisms since the end of the fourth century."

- St. Peter Julian Eymard preached extensively in the nineteenth century on the Eucharist and organized the Congregation of the Blessed Sacrament for men, and the Servants of the Blessed Sacrament for women. Fr. Hardon said St. Eymard's work was a great contribution "to a major development of doctrine in understanding the reality of Christ's Eucharistic presence now on earth."

- St. Alphonsus Liguori, an Italian bishop and theologian who founded the Congregation of the Most Holy Redeemer stated, "Our holy faith teaches us, and we are bound to believe, that in the consecrated Host, Jesus Christ is really present under the species of bread. But we must also understand that He is thus present on our altars as on a throne of love and mercy, to dispense graces and there to show us the love which He bears us, by being pleased to dwell night and day hidden in the midst of us." He is absolutely correct by saying that we must recognize that Jesus is "present on our altars." There he waits for our visits.

What a wonderful example of trust and prayer these witnesses to the faith have given us.

A Powerful Hour!

Venerable Archbishop Fulton Sheen, famous for his *Life is Worth Living* television series, used to spend at least an hour a day in Adoration of the Blessed Sacrament. He called it his "hour of power." He was convinced that he needed that time with Jesus to fulfill his responsibilities as a priest and archbishop. He said, "We become like that which we gaze upon, looking into a sunset, the face takes on a golden glow. Looking at our Eucharistic Lord for an hour transforms the heart in a mysterious way." The charismatic archbishop reflected on his daily Holy Hour in his autobiography, *A Treasure in Clay.* He said that Our Lord asked, "Could you not watch one hour with Me?" Ven. Sheen explained, "In other words, he asked for an hour of reparation to combat the hour of evil; an hour of victimal union with the Cross to overcome the anti-love of sin."

Ven. Sheen referred to the disciples falling asleep when Jesus was in his agony in the Garden. Jesus had asked Peter, James, and John to keep company with him. "As often in the history of the Church since that time, evil was awake," Archbishop Sheen explained. "But the disciples were asleep. That is why there came out of His anguished and lonely Heart the sigh: 'Could you not watch one hour with me?' Not for an hour of activity did He plead, but for an hour of companionship."

Ven. Sheen's explanation gives us reason to pause and ponder that sigh of Jesus, as well, and to endeavor to keep him company. He said, "The Eucharist is so essential to our one-ness with Christ that as soon as Our Lord announced It in the Gospel, It began to be the test of the fidelity of His followers." He explained, "First, He lost the masses, for it was too hard a saying and they no longer followed Him. Secondly, He lost some of His disciples: 'They walked with Him no more.' Third, it split His apostolic band, for Judas is here announced as the betrayer."

His time with Jesus in the Blessed Sacrament kept Ven. Sheen's "feet from wandering too far." No stranger to the darkness of the culture, he said, "The Holy Hour became like an oxygen tank to revive the breath of the Holy Spirit in the midst of the foul and fetid atmosphere of the world." Sometimes it was hard to persevere in prayer during his Holy Hours, especially when he was so tired. He said, "Even when it seemed so unprofitable and lacking in spiritual intimacy, I still had the sensation of being at least like a dog at the master's door, ready in case he called me."

This "saint" of the Holy Hour had much to say about that special hour of power. However, I'll leave you with this. He said:

> The purpose of the Holy Hour is to encourage deep personal encounter with Christ. The holy and glorious God is constantly inviting us to come to Him, to hold converse with Him, to ask for such things as we need and to experience what a blessing there is in fellowship with Him.[37]

Saint Joseph Pregnancy Prayer

Dear St. Joseph, though you remained quiet, you were very heroic and full of God's grace. You were ever attentive to the Holy Spirit and acted upon faith while courageously and lovingly caring for the Holy Family. The saints praise you as a powerful intercessor! St. Teresa of Avila said you never failed to help her. Please look kindly upon my cherished unborn grandchild and beseech our dear Lord to protect his or her precious life, as well as the life of his or her mother. Please help me to grow in holiness throughout this nine-month novena for my grandchild. Amen.

Memorare to Saint Joseph[38]

Remember, most pure spouse of Mary, ever Virgin, my loving protector, St. Joseph, that no one ever had recourse to your protection or asked for your aid without obtaining relief. Confiding, therefore, in your goodness, I come before you and humbly implore you. Despise not my petitions, foster-father of the Redeemer, but graciously receive them. Amen.

Memorare to Mary

Remember, O most gracious Virgin Mary, that never was it known that anyone who fled to thy protection, implored thy help, or sought thine intercession was left unaided. Inspired by this confidence, I fly unto thee, O Virgin of virgins, my mother; to thee do I come, before thee I stand, sinful and sorrowful. O Mother of the Word Incarnate, despise not my petitions, but in thy mercy hear and answer me. Amen.

Prayer to the Holy Family

Lord Jesus Christ, being subject to Mary and Joseph, you sanctified family life by your beautiful virtues. Grant that we, with the help of Mary and Joseph, may be taught by the example of your holy Family, and may after death enjoy its everlasting companionship. Lord Jesus, help us ever to follow the example of your Holy Family, that in the hour of our death your glorious Virgin Mother together with St. Joseph may come to meet us, and we may be worthy to be received by you into the everlasting joys of heaven. You live and reign forever. Amen.

To Ponder in Your Heart

Throughout this ninth month of your grandchild's development, do your best to slow down to ponder the words of Jesus, "And remember, I am with you always, to the end of the age" (Matthew 28:20). Take a moment to sincerely thank Jesus for this amazing gift! As well, ponder these words: "Could you not watch one hour with Me?" Consider striving to be more present to Jesus in your thoughts and prayers this month and allow him to be more present to you.

My reflections on being a Grandparent

The ninth month of pregnancy

Giving thanks to God for having created my grandbaby

A prayer in my own words

A Nine-Month Novena

To pray each day throughout this month

Dear Lord Jesus, Blessed Mother Mary, and all of the angels and saints, please hear my prayer. First, I desire to express my deep gratitude for the blessing of being chosen as a grandmother. I earnestly ask that while I pray for my precious unborn grandchild during this nine-month journey of growth in the womb, that you would watch over me and teach me. I desire to come ever closer to God so that I may become a dazzling example of Christian love to my grandchild—lighting the path to heaven. I pray that the love of God will continually radiate from my heart to touch the hearts of others, especially to all in my family. Thank you, dear Lord, for your abiding love! Amen.

My Grandchild's Birth Record

BABY'S NAME:

DATE OF BIRTH:

TIME OF BIRTH:

BABY'S WEIGHT:

BABY'S LENGTH:

FIRST IMPRESSIONS:

Prayer from my heart for my grandchild:

Popular Catholic Prayers

"For where two or three are gathered in my name,
I am there among them."
—MATTHEW 18:20

*I*t's so important to make the time to pray. God surely listens to all of our prayers whether formal or informal in our own words. Just a few words on prayer to open this Appendix of popular Catholic prayers:

Our prayers should always come forth from our sincere and humble hearts. Blessed Paul VI stated, "If you have lost the taste for prayer, you will regain the desire for it by returning humbly to its practice."[39]

The Catechism discusses prayer at length. When time allows, take a look to learn more. For now, be mindful that prayer needs to be an important part of our lives. St. Thérèse called prayer "a surge of the heart." She said, "For me, prayer is a surge of the heart; it is a simple look turned toward heaven, it is a cry of recognition and of love, embracing both trial and joy" (CCC #2558).

St. Augustine said, "Whether we realize it or not, prayer is the encounter of God's thirst with ours. God thirsts that we may thirst for him." It is amazing to ponder that God thirsts for our love. The Catechism also teaches that prayer ought to continuously animate our lives and the need to form what I call "prayer habits" (CCC #2697). We must make the time for prayer and strive to pray at specific times as well as to pray spontaneously as we offer our hearts to God like wafting holy incense making its way to heaven.

We mustn't ever give up on prayer, but rather, we should be patient with God and truly believe that he has our salvation in mind. If we were to receive everything we asked for in prayer, we might not make it to heaven. That might be a sobering statement. However, it is true. Let us wholeheartedly trust the Divine Physician, who knows exactly what we need and when we need it.

Jesus, I trust in You!

Prayer to Our Guardian Angel

Angel of God, my guardian dear, to whom God's love commits me here, ever this day be at my side to light and guard, to rule and guide. Amen.

Our Father

Our Father, who art in heaven, hallowed be thy name; thy kingdom come, thy will be done, on earth as it is in heaven. Give us this day our daily bread and forgive us our trespasses, as we forgive those who trespass against us and lead us not into temptation, but deliver us from evil. Amen.

Hail Mary

Hail Mary, full of grace, the Lord is with thee. Blessed art thou among women and blessed is the fruit of thy womb, Jesus. Holy Mary, Mother of God, pray for us sinners now and at the hour of our death. Amen.

Glory Be

Glory be to the Father, and to the Son, and to the Holy Spirit. As it was in the beginning, is now, and ever shall be, world without end. Amen.

Apostles' Creed

I believe in God, the Father almighty, creator of heaven and earth, and in Jesus Christ, His only Son, our Lord, who was conceived by the Holy Spirit, born of the Virgin Mary, suffered under Pontius Pilate, was crucified, died, and was buried. He descended into hell; the third day He rose again from the dead; He ascended into heaven and is seated at the right hand of the Father; from thence He shall come to judge the living and the dead. I believe in the Holy Spirit, the holy Catholic Church, the communion of saints, the forgiveness of sins, the resurrection of the body, and life everlasting. Amen.

Hail Holy Queen

Hail, Holy Queen, Mother of mercy, our life, our sweetness, and our hope. To thee do we cry, poor banished children of Eve. To thee do we send up our sighs, mourning and weeping in this vale of tears. Turn then, most gracious advocate, thine eyes of mercy towards us, and after this, our exile, show unto us the blessed fruit of thy womb, Jesus. O clement, O loving, O sweet Virgin Mary.

℣. Pray for us, O holy Mother of God.

℟.That we may be made worthy of the promises of Christ. Amen.

Prayer for a Family

Lord, bless our family, all of us now together, those far away, all who are gone back to you. May we know joy. May we bear our sorrows in patience. Let love guide our understanding of each other. Let us be grateful to each other. We have all made each other what we are. O family of Jesus, watch over our family. Amen.

Morning Offering

O Jesus, through the Immaculate Heart of Mary, I offer you all my prayers, works, joys and sufferings of this day, for all the intentions of your Sacred Heart, in union with the Holy Sacrifice of the Mass throughout the world, in reparation for my sins, for the intentions of all my relatives and friends and in particular of the Holy Father. Amen.

Grace Before Meals

Bless us, O Lord, and these thy gifts which we are about to receive from thy bounty. Through Christ Our Lord. Amen.

Prayer After Meals

We give you thanks for all your gifts, almighty God, living and reigning now and forever. Amen.

Evening Prayer

Hear us, Lord, and send your angel from heaven to visit and protect, to comfort and defend all who live in this house. Amen.

Family Prayer

O dear Jesus, I humbly implore you to grant your special graces to our family. May our home be the shrine of peace, purity, love, labor, and faith. I beg you, dear Jesus, to protect and bless all of us, absent and present, living and dead. Amen.

Prayer to Saint Michael the Archangel

St. Michael the Archangel, defend us in battle; be our defense against the wickedness and snares of the devil. May God rebuke him, we humbly pray, and do thou, O prince of the heavenly host, by the power of God, thrust into hell Satan and all the other evil spirits who prowl about the world seeking the ruin of souls. Amen.

Act of Contrition

O my God, I am heartily sorry for having offended Thee and I detest all my sins, because I dread the loss of heaven and the pains of hell, but most of all because they offend Thee, my God, who are all good and deserving of all my love. I firmly resolve, with the help of Thy grace, to confess my sins, to do penance, and to amend my life. Amen.

The Angelus

To commemorate the Incarnation, and to sanctify the hours of the day, echoing monastic prayer, the Angelus is prayed at 6 a.m., noon, and 6 p.m.

℣. The angel of the Lord declared unto Mary.

℟. And she conceived of the Holy Spirit. (Hail Mary . . .)

℣. Behold the handmaid of the Lord.

℟. Be it done unto me according to Thy word. (Hail Mary . . .)

℣. And the Word was made Flesh.

℟. And dwelt among us. (Hail Mary . . .)

℣. Pray for us, O holy Mother of God.

℟. That we may be made worthy of the promises of Christ.

Let us pray: Pour forth, we beseech Thee, O Lord, Thy grace into our hearts; that, we to whom the incarnation of Christ, Thy Son, was made known by the message of an angel, may by His Passion and Cross be brought to the glory of His Resurrection, through the same Christ, Our Lord. Amen.

Act of Family Consecration

Most Sacred Heart of Jesus and Immaculate Heart of Mary, we consecrate ourselves and our entire family to you. We consecrate to you: our very being and all our life. All that we are. All that we have. And all that we love. To you we give our bodies, our hearts and our souls. To you we dedicate our home and our country. Mindful of this consecration, we promise you to live the Christian way by the practice of Christian virtues, with great regard for respect for one another. O Most Sacred Heart of Jesus and Immaculate Heart of Mary, accept our humble confidence and this act of consecration by which we entrust ourselves and all our family to you. Most Sacred Heart of Jesus, have mercy on us. Immaculate Heart of Mary, pray for us. Amen.

Another Family Consecration

Jesus, Mary, Joseph! Graciously accept our family, which we dedicate and consecrate to you. Be pleased to protect, guard, and keep it in sincere faith, in peace and in the harmony of Christian charity. By conforming ourselves to the divine model of your family, may we all attain to eternal happiness. Amen.

Consecration to the Holy Family

O Lord Jesus,
you lived in the home of Mary and Joseph in Nazareth.
There you grew in age, wisdom and grace as you prepared to fulfill your mission as our Redeemer.
We entrust our family to you.

O Blessed Mary, you are the Mother of our Savior.
At Nazareth you cared for Jesus and nurtured him
in the peace and joy of your home.
We entrust our family to you.

O Saint Joseph, you provided a secure and loving home
for Jesus and Mary, and gave us a model of fatherhood
while showing us the dignity of work.
We entrust our family to you.

Holy Family,
we consecrate ourselves and our family to you.
May we be completely united in a love that is lasting,
faithful and open to the gift of new life.
Help us to grow in virtue, to forgive one another from our hearts,
and to live in peace all our days.
Keep us strong in faith, persevering in prayer,
diligent in our work, and generous toward those in need.
May our home, O Holy Family, truly become a domestic church
where we reflect your example in our daily life. Amen.
Jesus, Mary and Joseph, pray for us!

—Composed by Archbishop William E. Lori of Baltimore,
Supreme Chaplain of the Knights of Columbus[40]

Radiating Christ

St. John Henry Newman[41]

Dear Jesus, help me to spread Your fragrance everywhere I go. Flood my soul with Your Spirit and Life.

Penetrate and possess my whole being so utterly that my life may only be a radiance of Yours.

Shine through me and be so in me that every soul I come in contact with may feel Your presence in my soul.
Let them look up, and see no longer me, but only Jesus!

Stay with me and then I shall begin to shine as You shine, so to shine as to be a light to others.

The light, O Jesus, will be all from You; none of it will be mine.
It will be You, shining on others through me.

Let me thus praise You in the way You love best, by shining on those around me.

Let me preach You without preaching, not by words but by example, by the catching force, the sympathetic influence of what I do, the evident fullness of the love my heart bears for You. Amen.

Prayer to the Blessed Mother for family protection

ST. ALPHONSUS LIGUORI[42]

Oh Blessed and Immaculate Virgin, our Queen and Mother, refuge and consolation of all those who are in misery, I, prostrate before thy throne with all my family, choose thee for my Lady, Mother, and Advocate with God.

I, with all who belong to me, dedicate myself forever to thy service, and pray thee, oh Mother of God, to receive us into the number of thy servants, taking us all under thy protection, aiding us in life, and still more, at the hour of our death.

Oh Mother of Mercy, I choose thee Lady and ruler of my whole house, of my relatives, my interests, and all my affairs. Do not disdain to take care of them; dispose of them all as it pleases thee.

Bless me, then, and all my family, and do not permit that any of us should offend thy Son. Do thou defend us in temptations, deliver us from dangers, provide for us in our necessities, counsel us in our doubts, console us in afflictions, be with us in sickness, and especially in the agonies of death.

Do not permit the devil to glory in having in his chains any of us who are now consecrated to thee; but grant that we may come to thee in heaven to thank thee, and together with thee to praise and love our Redeemer Jesus for all eternity. Amen, thus may it be.

Anima Christi [43]

Soul of Christ, sanctify me.
Body of Christ, save me.
Blood of Christ, inebriate me.
Water from the side of Christ, wash me.
Passion of Christ, strengthen me.
O good Jesus, hear me.
Within Thy wounds, hide me.
Suffer me not to be separated from Thee.

From the malicious enemy, defend me.

In the hour of my death, call me and bid me come unto Thee,

that with Thy Saints I may praise Thee,

forever and ever. Amen.

Prayer for Grandchildren

Good Saint Anne and Saint Joachim,

parents of Mary and grandparents to Jesus,

be with me and all grandparents

that we may be wise and loving,

may share our time and stories and sense of humor,

and may enjoy and not spoil too much the grandchildren

who are close to our hearts,

for they are the sign of God's life to us.

Jesus, Mary and Joseph,

be with our grandchildren and all other grandchildren

that they may love and respect their grandparents

and all older people,

may remember to call,

visit or write,

and grow in wisdom,

age, and grace before God. Amen.

A Mother's Prayer to Her Children's Guardian Angels

I humbly salute you, O you faithful heavenly friends of my children! I give you heartfelt thanks for all the love and goodness you show them. At some future day I shall, with thanks more worthy than I can now give, repay your care for them, and before the whole heavenly court acknowledge their indebtedness to your guidance and protection. Continue to watch over them. Provide for all their needs of body and soul. Pray, likewise, for me, for my husband, and my whole family, that we may all one day rejoice in your blessed company. Amen.

Acknowledgments

I am deeply grateful to my parents, Eugene Joseph and Alexandra Mary Cooper, for bringing me into the world and raising me in a large Catholic family, and to my grandmother Alexandra Mary Uzwiak for setting a beautiful prayerful example. And thank you to my brothers and sisters—Alice Jean, Gene, Gary, Barbara, Tim, Michael, and David—for being a wonderful part of my life.

My heartfelt gratitude goes to my husband, Dave, and my beloved children—Justin, Chaldea, Jessica, Joseph, and Mary-Catherine—for their continued love and support, and to my precious grandsons, Shepherd and Leo. I love you all dearly.

I am deeply grateful to my friend, Servant of God Fr. John Hardon, SJ, who spiritually directed and encouraged me, and is no doubt continuing from heaven. Also, an exuberant thank you to dear Mother Teresa for playing a huge role in shaping me spiritually, which I know she continues even now, and to Fr. Andrew Apostoli, CFR, a dear friend and spiritual director, now helping me from heaven.

I owe very special thanks to Paraclete Press, to Jon Sweeney, and to Robert Edmonson, and all the wonderful team at Paraclete Press that helped get this book out to you!

Finally, I am extremely thankful for my readership, viewership, and listenership, and to all those I meet in my travels. I pray for you every day. Thank you for being part of my fascinating journey through life. Please pray for me, too. May God bless you in great abundance!

Notes

1 Saint Anne, Mother of the Blessed Virgin, EWTN online article, http://www.ewtn .com/library/mary/anne.htm.

2 Pius XII's radio message to schoolchildren: https://w2.vatican.va/content/pius-xii/en/ speeches/1958/documents/hf_p-xii_spe_19580219_alunni-usa.html.

3 Donald H. Calloway, MIC, *St. Joseph Gems* (Stockbridge, MA: Marian Press, 2018), 191.

4 *Favorite Prayers to St. Joseph* (Charlotte, NC: TAN Books, 1997), 6.

5 *Memorare* is a familiar form of prayer to Catholics. The word is Latin and means "Remember."

6 *Eat Less Cottage Cheese and More Ice Cream: Thoughts on Life from Erma Bombeck* (Kansas City, MO: Andrews McNeel Publishing, 2011), n.p.

7 Society of the Little Flower; https://www.littleflower.org/therese/life-story/her-parents/.

8 *Memorare* is a familiar form of prayer to Catholics. The word is Latin and means "Remember."

9 United States Conference of Catholic Bishops; http://www.usccb.org/prayer-and -worship/bereavement-and-funerals/blessing-of-parents-after-a-miscarriage-or-stillbirth.cfm.

10 Mary of Agreda, trans. Fiscal Marison, *The Mystical City of God: A Popular Abridgment of the Divine History and Life of the Virgin Mother of God* (Charlotte, NC: TAN Books, 1978), 39.

11 Mary of Agreda, *The Mystical City of God*, 57.

12 *Memorare* is a familiar form of prayer to Catholics. The word is Latin and means "Remember."

13 *Memorare* is a familiar form of prayer to Catholics. The word is Latin and means "Remember."

14 Mother Teresa, *Jesus: The Word to Be Spoken* (Ann Arbor: Servant Publications, 1986), n.p.

15 Franciscan Media blog; https://blog.franciscanmedia.org/franciscan-spirit/mother -teresa-on-mother-mary. Also Mother Teresa, *Thirsting for God: Daily Meditations*, ed. Angelo D. Scolozzi, MT (Cincinnati: Servant, 2000).

16 *Memorare* is a familiar form of prayer to Catholics. The word is Latin and means "Remember."

17 John Paul II, *Guardian of the Redeemer* (Boston: Pauline Books and Media, 2014), 20.

18 Fr. John A. Hardon, sj, "St. Joseph: Foster Father of Jesus," Fr. John A. Hardon, SJ Archive and Guild, https://hardonsj.org/foster-father-of-jesus-and-protector-of-the-virgin-mary/.

19 John Paul II, *Redemptoris Costus* (On the Person and Mission of Saint Joseph in the Life of Christ and of the Church), August 15, 1989; http://w2.vatican.va/content/john-paul-ii/en/apost_exhortations/documents/hf_jp-ii_exh_15081989_redemptoris-custos.html.

20 St. Joseph - Foster Father of Jesus, Fr. John A. Hardon, SJ Archives: http://www.therealpresence.org/archives/Josephology/Josephology_001.htm

21 *Saint Joseph the Worker, Man of Faith and Prayer,* 4. *L'Osservatore Romano,* Vatican, March 1983: https://www.catholicculture.org/culture/library/view.cfm?id=3329.

22 St. Teresa of Avila, *Autobiography of St. Teresa of Avila,* VI, 9 (Mineola, NY: Dover Publications, 2010).

23 *Memorare* is a familiar form of prayer to Catholics. The word is Latin and means "Remember."

24 Pope Benedict XVI, Angelus, March 27, 2011: http://w2.vatican.va/content/benedict-xvi/en/angelus/2011/documents/hf_ben-xvi_ang_20110327.html.

25 Saint Maria Faustina Kowalska, *Diary: Divine Mercy in My Soul* (Stockbridge, MA: Association of Marian Helpers, 2014), 146.

26 *Memorare* is a familiar form of prayer to Catholics. The word is Latin and means "Remember."

27 Tom Nash, *"Be Not Afraid!" 40 Years Later, National Catholic Register,* October 22, 2018; http://www.ncregister.com/blog/tom-nash/be-not-afraid-40-years-later.

28 His Holiness John Paul II, *Crossing the Threshold of Hope* (New York: Alfred A. Knopf, 1994), 218–19.

29 Saint Maria Faustina Kowalska, *Diary: Divine Mercy in My Soul,* 586.

30 George W. Kosicki, csb, and David Came, *John Paul II: The Great Mercy Pope* (Stockbridge, MA: Marian Press, 2011).

31 Saint Maria Faustina Kowalska, *Diary: Divine Mercy in My Soul,* 47, 48.

32 Saint Maria Faustina Kowalska, *Diary: Divine Mercy in My Soul,* 742.

33 *Memorare* is a familiar form of prayer to Catholics. The word is Latin and means "Remember."

34 Thomas Aquinas, *The Summa Theologica of St. Thomas Aquinas,* trans. Fathers of the English Dominican Province, June 1, 1981.

35 *The Real Presence of Jesus Christ in the Sacrament of the Eucharist: Basic Questions and Answers*, United States Conference of Catholic Bishops; http://www.usccb.org/prayer-and-worship/the-mass/order-of-mass/liturgy-of-the-eucharist/the-real-presence-of-jesus-christ-in-the-sacrament-of-the-eucharist-basic-questions-and-answers.cfm.

36 The quotes in this section are all taken from Fr. John A. Hardon, sj, "Eucharistic Saints"; http://www.therealpresence.org/archives/Saints/Saints_011.htm.

37 *Treasure in Clay: The Autobiography of Fulton Sheen* (San Francisco: Ignatius Press, 1980).

38 *Memorare* is a familiar form of prayer to Catholics. The word is Latin and means "Remember."

39 Bl. Paul VI, *EVANGELICA TESTIFICATIO*, 42: http://w2.vatican.va/content/paul-vi/en/apost_exhortations/documents/hf_p-vi_exh_19710629_evangelica-testificatio.html

40 "Consecration to the Holy Family," Knights of Columbus; http://www.kofc.org/en/programs/family/consecration-to-the-holy-family.html#/.

41 St. Teresa of Calcutta loved this prayer. The Missionaries of Charity pray it every day after receiving Holy Communion at Mass.

42 St. Alphonsus Liguori composed this prayer for families to dedicate themselves to the Virgin Mary, invoking her protection against all assaults of the devil.

43 This prayer originated in the fourteenth century and is usually prayed after receiving Holy Communion or after Mass, but it can be prayed anytime.

About Paraclete Press

WHO WE ARE

As the publishing arm of the Community of Jesus, Paraclete Press presents a full expression of Christian belief and practice—from Catholic to Evangelical, from Protestant to Orthodox, reflecting the ecumenical charism of the Community and its dedication to sacred music, the fine arts, and the written word. We publish books, recordings, sheet music, and video/DVDs that nourish the vibrant life of the church and its people.

WHAT WE ARE DOING

BOOKS | PARACLETE PRESS BOOKS show the richness and depth of what it means to be Christian. While Benedictine spirituality is at the heart of who we are and all that we do, our books reflect the Christian experience across many cultures, time periods, and houses of worship.

We have many series, including *Paraclete Essentials*; *Paraclete Fiction*; *Paraclete Poetry*; *Paraclete Giants*; and for children and adults, *All God's Creatures*, books about animals and faith; and *San Damiano Books*, focusing on Franciscan spirituality. Others include *Voices from the Monastery* (men and women monastics writing about living a spiritual life today), *Active Prayer*, and new for young readers: *The Pope's Cat*. We also specialize in gift books for children on the occasions of Baptism and First Communion, as well as other important times in a child's life, and books that bring creativity and liveliness to any adult spiritual life.

The MOUNT TABOR BOOKS series focuses on the arts and literature as well as liturgical worship and spirituality; it was created in conjunction with the Mount Tabor Ecumenical Centre for Art and Spirituality in Barga, Italy.

MUSIC | The PARACLETE RECORDINGS label represents the internationally acclaimed choir *Gloriæ Dei Cantores*, the *Gloriæ Dei Cantores Schola*, and the other instrumental artists of the *Arts Empowering Life Foundation*.

Paraclete Press is the exclusive North American distributor for the Gregorian chant recordings from St. Peter's Abbey in Solesmes, France. Paraclete also carries all of the Solesmes chant publications for Mass and the Divine Office, as well as their academic research publications.

In addition, PARACLETE PRESS SHEET MUSIC publishes the work of today's finest composers of sacred choral music, annually reviewing over 1,000 works and releasing between 40 and 60 works for both choir and organ.

VIDEO | Our video/DVDs offer spiritual help, healing, and biblical guidance for a broad range of life issues including grief and loss, marriage, forgiveness, facing death, understanding suicide, bullying, addictions, Alzheimer's, and Christian formation.

Learn more about us at our website
www.paracletepress.com
or phone us toll-free at 1.800.451.5006

SCAN
TO
READ

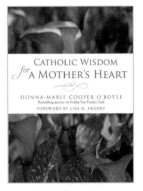
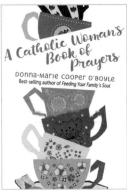